Apologetics

Never *Saved Anyone*

Fred DeRuvo

STUDY • GROW • KNOW

It's always time to study, grow and know your faith!

www.studygrowknow.com

Library of Congress Cataloging-in-Publication Data

DeRuvo, Fred, 1957 –

ISBN 0977424464
EAN-13 9780977424467

1. Religion – Christian Theology - Apologetics

Contents

Do not answer a fool according to his folly,

lest you yourself also be like him.

– Proverbs 26:4 (NET)

FOREWORD

Being a Christian is infinitely and eternally more than simply saying the words, "*I am a Christian.*" It means much more than just attending a Bible-believing church. It is so much more than reading the Bible, praying, and fellowshipping with others. Being a Christian *starts* with a *spiritual* transaction, which Christ has defined as a "new birth" in John 3. Being a Christian starts there, and continues from that point, and it only starts there through *faith*. Faith believes in God, His Word, His promises, His actions, and His atonement. Believing in spite of what circumstances try to tell us. Believing God's Word is true.

Without this spiritual transaction – what Christ also termed being "born again" in John 3, to a bewildered Nicodemus – there is *no* rebirth, and hence, no true Christianity. This is why in the parable of the sheep and the goats, Christ states there will be many who stand before Him in judgment, yet in spite of their belief about what they did, and what they said, the pronouncement of Christ counters all their protestations. "*Depart from me, I never knew you.*" These particular words are some of the most tragic words that Christ ever has to say, but the saddest part is that He actually says them to people who *think* beyond doubt that they *were/are* Christian! Either they did not know their true state, or they tried to impress Christ with what they did. What Christ is referring to here is being in relationship with Him. He is not talking about works, which people tend to believe save.

Works do *not* save. Attitudes do *not* save. Words do *not* save. The only thing that saves is faith, leading to the new birth. This spiritual transaction is something that occurs in the life of the sinner who comes to the point of realizing that his help comes only from somewhere outside of himself. He is unable to extricate himself from his own death and must therefore, rely on Someone outside of Himself. That Someone is Jesus.

It is only when the truth of who Jesus Christ is, shines into the heart of our soul, and we receive this truth, that the new birth occurs. This truth, then gives birth to life. That life is eternal life and since it is eternal, it can never be anything *but* eternal. Once a person truly *receives* the only salvation that is available through Jesus Christ, our Lord, then God moves him from the wide path that leads to destruction, placing him on the narrow path, which leads to life.

Christianity is *not* a religion. It is a *relationship* and that relationship is with God, the Son, who came in the form of humanity, lived among us, suffered as we suffer, and was tempted, as we are tempted. However, never in any moment of His entire earthly life did He ever succumb to any temptation to sin. In sinless perfection, He died a criminal's death on the cross in order to purchase for Himself a Bride.

It is only through our union with Him, through faith in the selflessness of His gracious act of death and resurrection that we participate with Him in life eternal. You cannot truly be a Christ "follower" unless you have a new birth. You honestly cannot *imitate* Him without His live within you. While it may appear to others that you are imitating Him, He will know whether your imitation of Him is outward, or from within. If it is from within, then it is true, because it stems from your relationship with Him. You can do all the 'good' things you want to do, but without a spiritual transaction, it all means absolutely nothing.

This book is a bit of a testimony of my own life along with an understanding of how He has worked within me over the years. The reality is that as I have grown in my faith, I have come to realize how much more I need to surrender to Him. This never-ending process takes our entire life to accomplish. However, even in that, we will never have fully arrived.

The narrow path, once found, is not without its hindrances. It is also not without its opportunities. The overall truth is that the narrow path is made up of stepping-stones and each of these stones brings us closer to leaving that much more of ourselves behind. As we walk the narrow path toward eternity, we shed layers of self. We learn that to enter into deeper relationship with Christ means to obey less and less of self's will and desires.

Losing self does not come about by *doing* things, or *saying* things, or even *thinking* things, unless the new birth has occurred. Losing self comes about only by giving up any rights we may think we have to our life. We begin to understand what Christianity means, when we begin to realize that His blood purchased us. Because we have been purchased, we are no longer our own. Our time does not belong to us. Our talents do not belong to us. Ultimately, our life does not belong to us. We need to be in the habit of living, not for ourselves, but for Him, in order that His purposes will come to fruition in and through us.

Tragically, now, more and more Christians are Christians in name only. As Paul would say, "Brothers, this ought not to be." We need to understand what it means to be a Christian. Once we begin to understand that, then our life will truly take on eternal meaning.

Fred DeRuvo, December 2009

Chapter 1

What Do You Know Anyway?!

GOOD-NATURED DEBATE IN THE TV LOUNGE

The room had gotten rather noisy. Here we were, sitting in the TV lounge of the school, watching the latest episode of M.A.S.H., when someone made the mistake of saying something that someone else disagreed with, and so it began. The volume level for the "discussion" quickly increased until it legitimately became a shouting match. I was one of those who had chosen to get my point across by using volume. It seemed like a good idea at the time. The one individual who had started the whole thing off remained rather calm about. That of course, simply made me increase my volume, since he was apparently not hearing me enough to be affected by what I was saying.

Finally, someone rather intelligently pointed out that we were in the TV lounge and we were there to watch M.A.S.H. Who could argue with that?

Later on, in my own room, I sat at my desk thinking about why I had responded the way I had responded. It was not merely me, but others had also reacted to the first individual's comment with rancor and even anger. At this point in my life – some thirty or so years later – I cannot even remember the subject of the brief argument. It really did not matter that much, except for the fact that I did not like to replay that memory in my head, complete with my own method of debate, which had been not only immature, but ineffective.

Of course, the answer came to me fairly quickly regarding why I had almost immediately responded with anger. I was insecure about my beliefs. Though there was little doubt as to *what* I believed, those beliefs were not as cemented as I would have liked them to have been. After all, I had a Bible degree from a very good school; a well recognized and respected college. I was now working on my M. Div degree at a seminary, which boasted very different beliefs than what I was used to appreciating. All of this made me question what I believed.

Being at this particular seminary caused me to question everything. Most people would say that was a good thing, because it caused me to stretch my thinking by questioning all that I had been taught. The result? I quit school, left the ministry in the dust, and got on with my life. For many years following, I simply "roamed." I do not mean roaming, as in moving from one place to the other. I mean, in my *mindset*, I could not get down to business. I could not – and did not – deal adequately with the issues that caused me to leave the seminary in the first place. Church became far less important for me and in fact, I did not really care if I attended any longer. It had become nothing more than something that people did on Sundays.

What I used to believe simply did not logically make sense to me (as if that was a prerequisite for understanding God's Word or His ways). I wound up moving from church to church, and never found anything that made me stand up and go, "*Wow! So THIS is what I've been missing all these years!*" There was nothing like that. I just floated, not all that concerned about the religious side of my life.

This went on for many years, even after I relocated back to California. After arriving and getting somewhat settled, I began to look for a church. I was not thinking about learning more about the Bible, or gaining closeness with God. I was more concerned about meeting people. After all, I was new to the area and wanted to get going with increasing my circle of friends, which at that point was a zero.

I began attending a church, and from there, I wound up going to a Bible study that took place on Tuesday evenings. There was another group from another church in attendance, which created a large group of Christians, with a variety of beliefs.

Eventually, as you may or may not guess, I met the woman who became my future wife through this Bible study, and after marriage, our life officially began together. One of the first things we did was to begin attending church together. The church I had been attending was the one we chose, due to its proximity to our apartment, but other than that, it had not really mattered to me where we went. Even at that, this church was a bit further than we liked. I just felt that it was important to go, even though most Sundays, I was so bored, every moment seemed like an hour. The only good thing about it was the fact that the pews were actually very comfortable!

WAYS TO GET OUT OF GOING TO CHURCH!

Eventually, we were tired of driving the distance to this church and found something a bit closer to us. It was within the same denomination, so we knew what they believed up front. We attended regularly, but suffice it to say, church was just not in me. My wife enjoyed it, to an extent. In fact, I was amazed how she always managed to get something out of the sermon, whereas I would often turn my brain off, having no real interest at all. I give her credit for being able to stay close to Him and His Word, in spite of the fact that I was not.

Eventually, we relocated to a town about three hours away and all things were new! There was a new house, new jobs, and new schools for the kids and of course, a new church.

We found one of those churches that happened to be a start-up church, meeting in a local high school on Sundays. We liked it. The music was good (it had a beat and you could dance to it), and the pastor's sermons (such as they were), were heavy on the "light" and filled with anecdotes and humor. Yep, just the thing to help stay awake!

Over time, this church continued to grow and then we began noticing some changes. The music started getting wild (I was a drummer on one of the worship teams), and the sermons became lighter and lighter. It was all a bit weird, frankly. We "toughed" it out until we could stand it no longer and we relocated again, this time to a church just up the street from us. It was a completely different denomination, but we felt comfortable enough with their statement of faith.

One thing I began to enjoy about this new church was the fact that they played hymns! Having been raised Baptist, it was a joy to sing those again, due to the tremendous amount of Scriptural truth found within the words. The sermons were normally very good. We enjoyed them.

Eventually (you knew that was coming), things began to change. One day, the hymns were noticeably gone, replaced with those upbeat choruses. The pastor's sermons started sounding more like history lessons – *boring* history lessons. I actually began bringing a book to church with me to read, can you believe that? This was appalling, but frankly, reading a Bill Bryson book was far more interesting than trying to get anything out of the sermons. I also brought religious type books to church with me on Sundays, which eliminated a bit of the guilt.

It was actually becoming painful for me to attend church. I would wake up on Sunday mornings, and pray that my wife would sleep too late for church! Alternatively, she might get up, but I would pretend to be asleep. When I did get up, I would move so slowly (you know, take a tremendously long time to read the paper, or hang out in my PJs, or become occupied with something that needed fixing), that I hoped she would get the message about me not wanting to go to church without having to ask me. That did not work. She always mentioned something about going to church.

As time went on, I began to feel as though my wife (get this), was trying to make me feel *guilty* for not wanting to go! I mean, after all, she would "henpeck" me (not really) every Sunday morning about going to church! I was having a very difficult time about wanting to go or not, and now here was my wife reminding me about going.

This all took a good deal of time to happen. It was not simply overnight that this occurred, but over a few years. However, it had gotten to the point where church and I just did not get along. On one hand, I did not want to go to church because it was so boring, but on the other hand, I was feeling guilty for not going because I thought I should. I was being emotionally crushed from both sides. It is interesting how the enemy of our souls works, is it not? First, he attempts to pull us away from God's will, then he turns around and attempts to make us feel guilty for not being involved in God's will!

Eventually, I went back to church. My wife and I worked out a deal. She would stop asking me, and I would not feel guilty if she went by herself. On top of that, I would try to get up the gumption to attend at least two Sundays a month. There, I did it! What a sacrifice I had made!

So life went on. I tried to keep my chin up and simply go to church, though I had actually gotten to a point where I hated it. I mean I did not like it at all. I felt that there was any number of valuable things I could be doing besides attending church. I could sleep in for one thing, or I could get up early and we could go to the beach, or a million other things besides. Going to church seemed like such a huge waste of time. What got me through was the fact that I brought a book with me to read...and sat somewhere toward the back, in order to make a quick escape (sometimes during the closing prayer).

Chapter 2

Surprised By a Thought

Cool!!

Things continued as they had for some time with respect to church. We went with my book in tow. At least it kept the annoyance at bay and off my face! When that happened, let me say that people do not have to guess what is going on in your mind. It is just way too obvious. The books kept me calm.

If you can try to appreciate the fact that I suffer from a bit of claustrophobia, you might have some sense of what was going on within me. Here I was, essentially forcing myself to be somewhere that I did not want to be. Couple that with the fact that I had to remain there for a certain period, because I was not allowed to leave, and you can see that one of the things I was fighting against was the desire to get up and run out of the place! I am not trying to make excuses. I am simply relating to you how I felt inside myself and why I wanted to run.

It was during one of these Sunday mornings while reading one of John MacArthur's books that a thought came. Now thoughts often come to me. Most thoughts, while interesting, leave as quickly as they arrive, merging into another thought, and then another and so on. My mind is always working.

At any rate, while reading one of Dr. MacArthur's books, I contemplated my life. I also remember praying, I mean just in case God was still interested in listening to my cares and concerns. I say that *not* because I believe that God came to the end of His patience with me, but because at that point in my life, I did not know whether He had. I figured there was a chance He was still being attentive, so why not? After all, I knew He could hear everything I thought, and saw everything I did anyway. The question was whether He chose to give me the time of day, because obviously, I had not been concerned about giving Him the time of day.

It was during one of these times in church, sitting there minding my own business, this thought came into my head that just about knocked me over. The thought was that I should go back and get my Masters degree in some area of Bible or Theology! Where did *that* come from and why did it come to me *now*, especially considering my thorough *lack* of interest up to that point? I quickly wrote a note to my wife and she looked at me with surprise and a smile.

As soon as we got home, I began searching the Internet for institutions that offered Masters Degrees in Bible or Theology. I quickly found a number of them, but most were way out of my ability to afford, or attend due, to distance.

I finally came across a number of schools that offered the ability to "attend" via the Internet. All work would be done at home on the computer and then submitted. I had the choice of either listening to the classroom lectures online, or at home via CD. I also could not believe how reasonably priced the tuition was for me! One of Tyndale's promises is to keep tuition as low as possible so that as many students as possible can avail themselves of the coursework. This means that the staff and instructors receive pay far below what might be considered acceptable, or the "norm" for college professors. They are not interested in making money. They are interested in providing a quality education at a more than fair price.

Therefore, for a few hundred dollars per course, the entire education cost around $4000. This is not a commercial for Tyndale, but simply an opportunity to point out that in spite of what some have stated or written about Tyndale, they are *not* there to take money and hand over a degree. They provide a quality education, at a very low cost.

Tentatively, I signed up for one course with Tyndale Theological Seminary based in Texas, and found to my delight, that I really enjoyed it. I was also quickly met with the reality that I knew far less than I thought I knew! This was not going to be easy. In fact, the very first class – in spite of all my effort and work – rewarded me with a grade of a "C." Not good. In spite of that, I decided to enter into a degree program and began in earnest to start working toward my Masters in Biblical Studies.

I could not believe how much work there was! Aside from listening to hours and hours of classroom lectures for each class, there were papers to write. The papers, for the most part, were at least 18 pages and some I submitted were as many as 65 pages or more! Whoever said that that studying online is a breeze has obviously never done it.

Roughly, 18 months later, I had submitted all coursework for each required course and had begun working on my oral exams, which would take place with a conference call. I had been provided the potential questions ahead of time. Since I was in the Masters program, the school provided me with a list of 150 questions that they could ask me during the conference call. Had I been going for my Doctorate, the quantity would have been 250! I studied and studied, jotted notes, created responses and ultimately wound up with nearly 100 pages of typed notes in preparation for the upcoming oral. I am happy to say that I passed the exam and am now the proud recipient of a Masters in Biblical Studies.

You may at this point be wondering what any of this has to do with apologetics and/or debate. We are going to get into that right now. I first wanted to provide a bit of background about myself. All of this plays an important part in the ongoing situation that many find themselves in today; namely debating aspects of theology.

It was not long after I received my degree that I began thinking about putting up my own web blog. After all, I had learned much (though there is always a great deal more to learn), and I felt there were some things I wanted to say about the Bible and theology.

Without hesitating, I created my own webpage and a blog. I wanted to get my thoughts out there and I wanted to see what other people were saying. Well, it was not long before I found out what people were saying and I did not like what I was reading at all.

Chapter 3

Who Would Have Thought?!

My first run in with an opposite viewpoint came shortly after I created my own blog. Things were going fine until happening upon a website, which attempted to analyze the area of Dispensationalism. Along with that, the Pretribulation Rapture position was high on their list of targets. Apparently, and unbeknownst to me, this particular position was more and more being seen as something that was akin to heresy. That certainly surprised me more than a bit, but I chalked it up to one individual and he was certainly entitled to his opinion. Moving along to other pages, it was not long before I came across other threads and pages, which showed a determined rancor where Dispensationalism was concerned. This was becoming troubling, not because these people's opinions bothered me, but because they did not seem to have a correct understanding on what Dispensationalism wall all about.

I read incorrect assumption after incorrect assumption and it began to get on my nerves. I had just acquired a Masters degree in Biblical Studies, and while I was not an expert, I was keenly aware of the fact that the Dispensationalism that people were commenting on was *not* the Dispensationalism with which I was familiar. The more I read, the more incredulous I became toward these opinions.

In fact, I quickly realized that simply writing a blog about it would not really serve my purposes. For one thing, it would take an extremely large blog to note all of the misconceptions about Dispensationalism and then address them. No one would want to read a blog *that* long. Secondly, I realized just how badly people seemed to *hate* the topic of Dispensationalism, and those who espoused it.

I spent some time on forums watching and reading the discussions, which more often than not turned very quickly into raging debates, with uncharitable words being written back and forth. Eventually, as you might guess, the moderators or administrators would have to step into a thread, give a warning, and then eventually lock the thread if the warning was not obeyed. The amount of vitriol, rancor, and toxic verbiage exchanged was unbelievable. It should not be the case with Christians. However, who is to say who is really a Christian by simply reading their words on a forum? I had long ago realized that some people go from forum to forum for one purpose and one purpose only, which is to incite. They do this to get people at each other's throats. Then, they simply sit back and enjoy what they have created. It is kind of like an arsonist. He tosses a lit match onto a fuel source, then watches with twisted delight the conflagration that follows. It gives him a thrill he can get in no other way.

People who go from forum to forum do the same thing by inciting arguments. Commonly referred to as *trolls,* these folks do not even care what they themselves believe. What matters to them is making instigating comments that will simply serve to ignite the flames of passion and anger. Once they have successfully done that, they lean back in their easy chair, with a bowl of popcorn and a soda, and they are entertained.

Of course, not all people on forums do this, but it is rare to read words like *"I could be wrong, but my opinion on this is..."* Normally, what is stated is much more akin to *"No, that is NOT what the Bible says, moron! You would think someone who actually professed to be a Christian would have some basic understanding of how to rightly interpret Scripture!"* Then someone else comes back with a similar comment and things are off and running! The "discussion" has turned into a debate, complete with castigating and denigrating comments and lectures, directed to force the other individual into full submission. At times, even moderators and administrators can be just as bad. Their position goes to their heads and in their arrogance, they tend to run roughshod over people, doing whatever it takes to enforce their rules.

It was not long before I swore off forums. Not once did I ever read words that were mildly charitable, with a give and take attitude associated with them. Instead, just about any subject somewhere turned into an argument and it did not matter what the subject was about either.

I began to read more books on varying theological viewpoints and I often came away with the same opinion. I was appalled to read opinions couched with vitriolic verbiage. It is incredible how spiteful people can be toward those who do not share their opinions. Where were the Ryries, the Walvoords, and the other people who express their opinion *and* their disagreement with another individual, in *charitable terms*? It was almost as if Christians had come to the point of thinking that as long as you believed you were defending God's Word, anything goes. In fact, name-calling had obviously become a normal way of offering an opinion. Someone offered an opinion, while at the same time, those opposed to that opinion were referred to in a derogatory manner. They would also be attacked verbally.

The reality is that what I began to uncover was a no-holds barred form of debating. There was *no* discussion. It was all slamming one opinion down someone else's throat. The idea was to beat the other person over the head with a Bible, a commentary, or just an opinion, and do it until the other person cried "Uncle!" At that point, the "victor" *might* ease up, let the other person go and move on to the next contender.

Civility had literally gone the way of the dinosaur, having become virtually extinct. I have to admit that I can be as sarcastic as the next person. It is very easy to lower myself to that level, and for some reason, it seems to spill out of me naturally. (Gee, I wonder if the sin nature has anything to do with that?) Left unchecked, this can easily become a normal way of communicating. However, is it Scriptural? Is it the way in which Jesus Himself communicated? Most would agree that it is not.

One thing I noticed was that it became much easier for people to condemn the viewpoints of others if they were seen as *heretics*. Once classified as believing and espousing aberrant doctrine, a person *ceases* to be a person. They become someone standing against Jesus Christ and the Truth of His Word. Because of that, it becomes a righteous and holy war – us against them, truth against error. The trouble of course, is that Paul tells us that we do not wrestle against flesh and blood but against the principalities and powers in the spiritual realm (cf. Ephesians 6:12). Do we stop to consider what that actually means? Most of the time, it is obvious that we do not, seeing the other person as the enemy.

Chapter 4

It's the Debate, Stupid!

The more books I read, the more disgusted I became. The more blogging I created, the less I felt like blogging, or even talking with anyone else about a theological opinion he might not share. People would read a blog post and then respond with sarcasm, fury, antagonism and more, in an attempt to get their point across. What had become of any semblance of civility? It seemed that like chivalry, it was gone, never to return. However, there was also something more troubling that I began to notice. I started to see something else at work, something below the surface, which to my mind appeared to be the all-encompassing reason why people responded as they did. It can be summed up in one word: *debate*.

People appeared to be much more interested in *debating* than in *discussing*. I had to ask why? The answer came through a series of emails I had with several individuals with whom I did not (and do not) agree theologically. In the few email discussions we had, no amount of evidence would show he held an errant theological position. I am sure they would say the same thing about me as well.

That aside, *both* individuals at one point in the exchange of emails, bragged about never *losing a debate*. I thought that was interesting to say the least. In fact, one of the individuals went so far as to point out that he had never lost a debate, *nor* had a friend of his. Hmmm. That made me think, and I began to realize that for some people, winning the debate was obviously *the* reason to interact with others. For them, winning was everything.

It turned out that this certainly seems to be true, when two or more people are involved in some type of — what starts out to be — religious discussion. Some people are surreptitious about the whole debate thing, preferring to come across as someone who simply wants to "discuss." They will attempt to persuade with every form of guilt cue, or compliment — whatever it takes to get you drawn into the thick of it. Why? Because apparently, folks like these have this tremendous desire to prove other people *wrong*. The more people they feel they can prove to be incorrect, the more they will come to think of themselves as being correct, and the more their self-esteem is improved. It is a vicious cycle because these folks seem not to care about the people to which they are opposed. What matters to them is making sure that the other person sees just how incorrect they truly are about some aspect of theology.

What I have come to realize though, is that while all Christians need to know *what* they believe, and *why* they believe it, I do *not* see a need to enter into a *debate* with someone over this issue or that. The reason is mainly that I do not see that Jesus did this either. Paul, while attempting to convince, certainly knew when to stop, unlike many people today.

Now someone might come along and insist that the people who are hearing the debate (or reading it, if it is online), benefit from it because those who have not made up an opinion, might be able to do so. This is not really accurate, because it all depends upon the issue and the amount of knowledge each individual debater possesses.

Some folks have a great wealth of information at their fingertips that they can recall on a dime. They may *appear* to be the better-informed individual, and on that alone, may wind up bringing undecided folks around to their opinion. This does not mean that they have the truth. It may simply mean that they *come across* more intelligently than the other person they are debating.

Some people are winsome, upbeat, intelligent-sounding, or have an air of charisma that makes people want to believe them. This however, does not mean they have the truth. It simply means they are winsome, upbeat, intelligent-sounding, and have air of charisma that attracts people to them. Because of that, people are willing to overlook obvious faults or inconsistencies because they want so much to believe that person.

This type of thing goes on all the time during political primaries and elections. For too long it has been nothing more than a favored personality contest, as opposed to seeing past the personality, in order to determine the true substance of promises made on the campaign trail. Personality and the many things go with personality, do not make truth apparent. In fact, this type of personality can and often does, *hide* the truth, in favor of pushing an agenda that is far from the truth. In my opinion, this is exactly what happened with the election of our current president.

Just because someone debates a subject well, does not again mean that truth is on his or her side. Currently, it has become all too prevalent to declare one's self the winner of a debate by popularity alone, or worse, by that individual's own assessment of things. This is disadvantageous to those who really want to know the truth.

Show me a debate where those debating come to the debate already being fully convinced of their own opinion, and I will show you a discussion in which no one's opinion is changed, and people simply wind up talking to hear themselves talk.

In today's world, debating is more of an exercise in *entertainment* than anything. The more I study the Word, the more convinced I am that debating is not something that Jesus engaged in, and for worthy reasons.

At times, Christians *should* engage in apologetics. In fact, every time a Christian witnesses to a lost individual, apologetics plays a part. We *explain* why Jesus is the only way to heaven, and *how* salvation is available in and through Him. We do this, not by trying to convince them with great-sounding human arguments, but by using Scripture, showing how God in Christ came to die, in order that we might live.

In the process of witnessing to people, we may choose to start with the third chapter of the gospel of John, or the first and second chapters of Romans, or somewhere else entirely. The main thing is in showing a person *why* they need salvation in the first place, and *how* they can receive it.

Years ago, much of what went on as debate in the religious arena was usually relegated to proving God existed, or Creation vs. Evolution. Over time, more and more debate has shifted to the entire arena of religious topics:

- Israel vs. the Church
- Dispensationalism vs. Covenantalism
- The meaning of Christianity
- The dating of the book of Revelation
- Whether or not Christ returned in A.D. 70

Besides the topics noted above, people argue and debate over many areas within the realm of religion. The question is, *why* is this true? Does debating help people arrive at a solution? Not from what I have seen. More often than not debating simply pits one person against another person often taking on a *personal* agenda. Debates can and do often become mean-spirited, quickly escalating from a simple and even congenial discussion, to a war of words. When it reaches that point, the ad hominem comments are usually in full force.

This is the problem with debating. We learn something and we quickly think we have become experts. We then feel we must share what we know with anyone who will listen. After all, we muse, it is for their own good. They need to hear the truth. Well, in fact, the main truth that people *need* to hear is that Jesus is "the Way, the Truth and the Life" and that "no one comes to the Father except through" Him (cf. John 14:6). This again is not to minimize other important doctrines like the Tri-unity of the Godhead, the deity of Christ, the fact of the resurrection of Jesus, the truth that Jesus was and remains fully God and fully Man.

There are many doctrines of the faith that we *should* know and believe, however if you had only one portion of the Scriptures that you could take with you as you evangelized the lost, would you not want portions of Scripture that dealt with the fact of Jesus as Savior of the world?

Chapter 5

You Sir, Are a Heretic!

Heretic is a word that you hear a great deal today. More and more, people are either calling someone else a heretic or they hear it applied to them. Why? Because somewhere along the line, something you believe to be true about the Bible is at odds with what someone else believes about the Bible (or is actually at odds with the Bible itself), and the result after discussing it, and not be able to resolve it, is to label them a heretic.

When we label people heretics, we instantly remove their humanity. They become less than human, and much more devilish. Because he is now part of the ranks of the deceived and deluded, we feel no pity or compassion for them. Because of that, anything goes. In fact, the worse they appear to us, the easier it is to haul them over the coals.

Is this not what Jesus did with the Pharisees? He *more* than scolded them. He held nothing back when dealing with the Pharisees! He pointed out their flaws and failures to understand God's Word, as *God* meant it, and He did this repeatedly. Time after time, Jesus dealt with the problem directly, and embarrassed the religious leaders in front of their flock. The Pharisees and teachers of the Law simply could not refute or even stand up under Christ's flawless insight and delivery.

Argument after argument was lost at the feet of Jesus and the Pharisees were left standing there, smoldering in their sandals. Frankly, those

SORE LOSERS OF THE FIRST CENTURY

poor, abused Pharisees were sick and tired of it. Now in today's world, we resort to name-calling. That is how we "kill" our foes. Sometimes, we do it smoothly, like a gentleman from the Victorian Age who might state, *"Why Percy, old man, the very fact that you have arranged to come to a gentleman's disagreement bearing nothing but a smile and a handkerchief does not bode well for one such as yourself, who might be classified as neither a scholar, nor a gentleman."*

To the above, Percy might offer, *"Ah, my dear Boris, you've certainly cut me to the quick. However, the truth of the matter will shortly be seen when all of your remonstrance will be known for what it is; abject poverty. The most difficult aspect of this upcoming discussion will be in my own ability to reign in the desire to completely annihilate you verbally."*

Both men of course, would say these things with smiles on their faces and once each has offered his very best rejoinder, both men would shake hands, and leave the other with a comment similar to, *"Please give my regards to your lovely bride. I have always admired your taste in the fairer sex."* The other would offer, *"Why it pleases me to know that you think so. And may I say that your wife is a true feast for the eyes, lighting up every room she walks into with the beauty of her smile."*

Certainly, no one would argue with the statement that those days are clearly gone and gone for good. Politeness and what could be termed charity, is something that rarely seen in debates at all today. None of this should be surprising however, as we are very likely reaching the close in what most conservative Bible scholars believe to be the Last Days, or End Times. Because of this, both Paul and Peter explain to us what to expect from the demeanor of human beings, both in and out of the visible Church during this time.

"But know this, that in the last days grievous times shall come. For men shall be lovers of self, lovers of money, boastful, haughty, railers,

disobedient to parents, unthankful, unholy, without natural affection, implacable, slanderers, without self-control, fierce, no lovers of good, traitors, headstrong, puffed up, lovers of pleasure rather than lovers of God; holding a form of godliness, but having denied the power therefore," (2 Timothy 3:1-5, ASV).

"But there were also false prophets among the people, just as there will be false teachers among you. They will secretly introduce destructive heresies, even denying the sovereign Lord who bought them—bringing swift destruction on themselves. Many will follow their shameful ways and will bring the way of truth into disrepute. In their greed these teachers will exploit you with stories they have made up. Their condemnation has long been hanging over them, and their destruction has not been sleeping," (2 Peter 2:1-3, ASV).

Chapter 6

When Winning is Everything

NO ONE LIKES TO LOSE...

I WON!!

I HATE YOU!

©2009 F. DERUVO

"I have never lost a debate with a 'pretribber' and neither has...any other qualified individual."

I received the above quote in an email. Stated comments like these come from people who believe they not only have the Truth, but to disagree with them means that you are fighting against God. Moreover, those who make the type of statement noted above base their comment on an invisible determiner of who wins what debate. In other words, if two people are debating, it is very possible that *both* will tell you they won the debate. What does that actually mean though? How is it *determined* who wins a debate?

Obviously, if one of the individuals in a debate has no response, hems and haws a good deal, or stutters and splutters, sweating profusely as he searches in vain for a response to his inquisitor, then the chances are great that people will proclaim this individual the loser of the debate. The other person walks away from the podium, doing their best to hide their Cheshire grin, while trying to act humbly.

What does it actually mean to say, "I won" when referencing a debate that has just ended? Does it not mean *only* that the person who allegedly lost the debate may not have known as much, or able to present the information as flawlessly? Does that mean that the alleged winner actually has the *truth* in that given situation? Maybe not, as it may mean that the "winner" was the best debater...for that event.

This is the tragedy of traveling down the debate road. An individual of a debate is the crowned winner, though he may have the furthest thing from what is *actual* truth. Winning a debate alone is not enough to prove that the truth has in actuality, been espoused. What is necessary is to *know* that what is stated *is,* in fact, *the truth.* This only occurs when people humbly approach God's Word, with a supreme desire to seek His wisdom in all things.

It also forces us to ask the question . . . what have we gained by "winning" the debate, especially if we consider the fact that we may or may not have the truth?

Chapter 7

What Does the Bible Say?

The most important thing we can do as we search for our answer to the question of debating, is to go to the Scriptures. In it, we will see if people spent their time debating and arguing, or if they simply presented the information that God provided, leaving it hanging in the air. Once out there, it then becomes the responsibility of each listener to decide for him or herself what they will do with that truth.

There are many places in the Bible where we can begin, as we search for the answer to this entire question of debating. The book of Proverbs seems a logical place to look.

Solomon, who was undoubtedly the wisest man who ever walked this earth, apart from Jesus Himself, filled volumes with idioms, and sayings that address many aspects of life. He speaks of *actively* seeking wisdom above all things, and in every situation, that life presents.

Part of Proverbs 9:7-10 (NASB) states,

> *"He who corrects a scoffer gets dishonor for himself,*
> *And he who reproves a wicked man gets insults for himself.*
> *Do not reprove a scoffer, or he will hate you,*
> *Reprove a wise man and he will love you.*
> *Give instruction to a wise man and he will be still wiser,*
> *Teach a righteous man and he will increase his learning.*
> *The fear of the Lord is the beginning of wisdom,*
> *And the knowledge of the Holy One is understanding."*

This truth is simple to appreciate and it speaks to the one who wants to enter into debate with another. Solomon highlights four things here:

1. Choose carefully whom you will correct
2. Scoffers are too proud to admit when they might be wrong
3. Wise individuals are wise in part because they *receive* correction
4. A proper fear of the Lord, causes us to be certain that what we teach and preach is actually what the Lord teaches

How does this apply to the world of debating? First, it actually *precludes* continuous debating for the sole reason that normally, both individuals are set in their beliefs and they are out to prove that the other individual is completely wrong. Both individuals consider themselves wise, learned, and they do not believe they can learn anything from the other person.

Besides this, even if there is a fair way to determine who actually wins a debate, has anyone ever heard of the "loser" being turned to the other individual's position? It is unheard of within the confines of debating. That is not its function. Debating serves one purpose and one purpose only; to prove that the position one individual holds is the correct and therefore superior position. There is no give and take in debating. One person presents an argument. The other person responds in an effort to negate that first argument, while furthering his own. Based on this, a winner is "declared."

Yet, Proverbs 9 states clearly that if someone corrects another person who is already scoffing at his or her position, the person doing the correcting is dishonored. Why is that the case? The scoffer's tendency is to *rebuke* the wiser person, normally with *ridicule*. This is often normally the result, and it is fast becoming the norm, even outside the formal arena of debate.

Think of any debate that you may have watched, listened to, or read (on a forum for instance). It does not take long for the debate to reduce itself into a litany of caustic or sarcastic comments, designed not to respond with fact, but merely to simply castigate.

I recall one of the debates between two vice presidential candidates a number of years ago. Dan Quayle was at one podium, with Lloyd Bensen on the other. We all know that these individuals had practiced debating in days prior to this actual televised debate. It would be stupid not to use the time preceding the debate for practice and research. During those practice debates, certain questions would be posed, with potential answers given. There would also be situations in which one candidate would look for a possible "hole" where he could lambaste his opponent's opinion, not with any pertinent facts necessarily, but with an opportunity to ridicule.

Such an opening occurred during the debate when Dan Quayle made the mistake of mentioning President John F. Kennedy. He did so in an appropriate manner, calling attention to the fact that he (Quayle) had as much political experience as the late president. One of his biggest hurdles was the fact that critics and political pundits alike were claiming that because of Quayle's lack of experience in the political arena, he was unqualified to be vice president.

What Quayle did was merely compare the *amount* of political experience he had with the *amount* of experience Kennedy had when Kennedy ran for president. Whether true or not, the point was completely lost when Bensen responded with, *"Senator, I served with Jack Kennedy. I knew Jack Kennedy. Jack Kennedy was a friend of mine. Senator, you're no Jack Kennedy."*[1] What did *not* matter was that Bensen's comment was unimportant and ultimately, off-topic, since Quayle's only comparison with Kennedy was the amount of *experience*, not character or any other attribute. Possibly a nicer way to say what Bensen said, might have been something like *"Senator, length of experience does not necessarily equate to quality of experience."*

Unfortunately, this was a climax in the debate as the reaction of the live audience proved. There was nothing for Quayle to do except point out that the comment from Bensen had been unnecessary. In fact, it was unnecessary and rude. Nevertheless, that did not matter, because in debating, what often seems best is to resort to the *ad hominem* argument, which simply attacks the individual, instead of addressing any differing points. This is what debating has become and it is obvious, because of stand-up comedians, sitcoms and all the "talking heads" or news pundits and commentators that people in general have lowered themselves to the worst common denominator, which is to cut down opponents, instead of actually speaking *to* the issues. Even when just

---

[1] http://en.wikipedia.org/wiki/Lloyd_Bentsen

the issues are actually being debated, debates still tend to wind up solving nothing, and swaying no one.

In the book of Ezekiel, we read of God's call of the prophet Ezekiel, in which God chose him to relay messages to the nation of Israel. He did this not only in *words*, but also in *actions*. In chapter one of Ezekiel, the prophet is shown numerous events in which he sees visions of angels that have four faces, and four wings, which allows them to go in any direction instantly, without turning. He sees visions of divine glory above these angels and finally, in chapter two, Ezekiel receives his call from God Himself. Ezekiel's call is very interesting.

As God calls the prophet, He states (2:3-6, NET), "*Son of man, I am sending you to the house of Israel, to rebellious nations who have rebelled against me; both they and their fathers have revolted against me to this very day. The people to whom I am sending you are obstinate and hard-hearted, and you must say to them, 'This is what the sovereign Lord says.' And as for them, whether they listen or not – for they are a rebellious house – they will know that a prophet has been among them. But you, son of man, do not fear them, and do not fear their words – even though briers and thorns surround you and you live among scorpions – do not fear their words and do not be terrified of the looks they give you, for they are a rebellious house!*"

Please note that God already knows the condition of the house of Israel and He knows whether they will receive the prophet's words. In fact, in verse seven, the LORD states, "*You must speak my words to them **whether they listen or not**, for they are rebellious.*" (emphasis added)

Notice that God does not indicate to Ezekiel that the prophet will be able to *convince* Israel of anything, or that this is even part of Ezekiel's task. God is warning him that regardless of the nation's response, as a prophet that God has called, Ezekiel's responsibility is to say what God tells him to say. He is *not* responsible to convince them of anything.

GOD INSTRUCTS EZEKIEL ABOUT ISRAEL

EZEKIEL! TELL THEM WHETHER THEY LISTEN OR NOT!

YES, LORD

©2009 F. DERUVO

God did not say, "*I want you to enter into debate with them, and I will provide you with the words that will convince them of their error.*" There is nothing like that at all. God simply states that the prophet must do the job that God has called him to do. The outcome is not in Ezekiel's hands, nor is it part of his job description.

Throughout the entirety of the book of Ezekiel, God comes to him at various points and tells him what to do and/or what to say. There were some very interesting things required of Ezekiel. God designed these things in order to get the point across to Israel. God tells Ezekiel to eat a scroll (cf. 2:8-10), stating, "*Son of man, feed your stomach and fill your body with this scroll which I am giving you,*" (Ezekiel 3:3, NASB). This is not only God's Word to Ezekiel, but it is God's Word to us. We are to fill ourselves with His Word, so that it is literally *part* of us. If we *never* read the Bible, or study it, it will never become part of us. We will never have anything to draw on during those times when we are in situations, which require the knowledge, strength, and truth of His Word.

God told Ezekiel to *feed* on His Word. The truth that *is* God's Word is to be our sustenance. This is exactly why Jesus could say to His disciples that He had *food* they did not know of, which was to do the will of Him who sent Jesus (cf. John 4:1-48). God's Word is *food*. It is *life* and to ignore it means to starve to death spiritually, from lack of sustenance. Our Christian lives will quickly become hollow, shallow, and superficial. Carnal living is not far behind.

God warns Ezekiel against this by telling him to eat the scroll and feed on it. Ezekiel ate it and testified that it was sweet in his stomach (cf. 3:3).

Throughout the book of Ezekiel, God comes to the prophet with new information and new explanations about what He is going to do in and through the nation of Israel. God says He is going to judge Israel because of the evil in their life, as a nation. It is important to note that when God looked upon the nation of Israel, He did so as a nation. If only one person acted with evil intentions, the entire nation suffered the consequences of those actions. Joshua chapter seven is merely one example of this rule. Even in spite of the righteous people living in Israel at the time, God indicated that His judgments would fall on the entire nation because of their perverseness. On one particular occasion in the ninth chapter of Ezekiel, one of the angels out of the six present, is told to go through Israel and *"put a mark on the foreheads of the men who sigh and groan over all the abominations which are being committed in its midst,"* (cf. 9:4). These men were spared execution by the other angels, whose job it was to follow the first angel, and destroy all who did not have the mark. This was done in order for God to keep a remnant of believers for Himself, so that the entire nation of Israel was not blotted out.

What the LORD showed Ezekiel time after time were events and situations, which were reprehensible to God. He did not overlook, but with patience, allowed the Israelites to continue in the hopes of eventually seeing repentance. This should warn us of our own idolatry and failure to obey God in all things. Are our own lives *right* with God? Do we confess our sin as quickly as He brings it to our attention, or do we treat sin as if it is no big deal, and nothing to worry over?

When you read the book of Ezekiel, you find it incredible that our holy God would put up with the evil that Israel evidenced time after time. Yet, this is what occurred, as they mixed pagan worship with worship of the One, True God.

As God takes Ezekiel through various parts of the Temple for instance, the prophet witnesses the things that the elders of Israel are committing in the dark, thinking God does not see. God asks Ezekiel, *"Son of man, do you see what the elders of the house of Israel are committing in the dark, each man in the room of his carved images?"* These elders were guilty of doing this in God's very Temple! Is it any wonder that God would not – *could* not – enter the Temple that had originally been dedicated to him, because it had become a Temple of Satan?

Had Ezekiel explained why these things were wrong to these elders (they already knew that), and tried to convince them that they needed to repent, the outcome would have been no different from what we read in the book. Numerous times, God sent foreign enemies of Israel to rebuke and chastise them, often allowing these enemies to slaughter them, leaving only a few to carry on the nation of Israel. When God's anger and wrath and been expended, He began to once again, pick up the pieces and would slowly call the remaining Israelites back to His Land.

No amount of debate with the elders or other leaders of Israel would have amounted to anything. Ezekiel's job was to pronounce and announce. It was not to enter into debates with the elders, or the priests. His job was not to convince them that they were wrong or that they needed to change their attitudes about sin. Ezekiel's job was to *inform* the nation (through the leaders), of God's impending judgment. Yes, he was to tell them to repent, but there is no indication in the entire book that he could *convince* them to do that. In fact, God's initial words *"whether they listen to you or not,"* precludes the concept of debating with them.

Ezekiel's responsibilities included *telling* Israel of the problem, in whatever way God determined that Ezekiel should speak or show it. He was to make them completely aware of the things that brought God to a point where judgment seemed to be the only solution to the problem of the Israelites. In fact, God warned Ezekiel throughout the book, that if he *failed* to warn them and someone died in their sin and unright-eousness, while they would be held accountable for their own sin, Ezekiel's blood would also be required, because he had failed as a prophet (cf. 3:16-21; 33:6,8). This was the extent of his responsibilities. Nowhere he is told to debate, or attempt to *convince* Israel of their problem and the solution. He is to inform. Whether or not Israel listened was not Ezekiel's responsibility.

However, what about debating in today's culture? Somewhere along the line, we have adopted the opinion that if we could but convince someone that he is wrong and we are right, then we will have accomplished something. In truth though, what have we actually accomplished? Debating is often done to promote someone's opinion over someone else's opinion. As previously stated, the "winner" of a debate might still be the loser, if they do not have the truth. In that case, not only has nothing been gained, but ground has been lost.

Chapter 8

What **Did** Jesus Do?

Without doubt, in determining whether or not debating an issue has any real merit, we must consider the life of Christ and His responses to those who opposed Him. Though we do not have record of Christ dealing with every possible topic, we *do* know how He handled the topics that came His way. It is important for us to understand not only *how* Jesus responded in specific situations, but *why* He responded as He did. Did Jesus *debate*, or did He simply *state*? Let us take some time to find out.

The first time we read of Jesus being involved in any discussion was when He was but a young boy of twelve. The account is detailed for us in the gospel of Luke and while there is not a tremendous amount there, we certainly see enough.

> "Now Jesus' parents went to Jerusalem every year for the feast of the Passover. When he was twelve years old, they went up according to custom. But when the feast was over, as they were returning home, the boy Jesus stayed behind in Jerusalem. His parents did not know it, but (because they assumed that he was in their group of travelers) they went a day's journey. Then they began to look for him among their relatives and acquaintances. When they did not find him, they returned to Jerusalem to look for him. After three days they found him in the temple courts, sitting among the teachers, listening to them and asking them questions. And all who heard Jesus were astonished at his understanding and his answers. When his parents saw him, they were overwhelmed. His mother said to him, "Child, why have you treated us like this? Look, your father and I have been looking for you anxiously." But he replied, "Why were you looking for me? Didn't you know that I must be in my Father's house?" Yet his parents did not understand the remark he made to them. Then he went down with them and came to Nazareth, and was obedient to them. But his mother kept all these things in her heart. And Jesus increased in wisdom and in stature, and in favor with God and with people." (Luke 2:41-52, NET)

We see a number of things in this section of Scripture that show us Jesus' deportment and attitude toward discussion. Here, Jesus' parents had been looking for Him, and after three days, they found Him sitting in the Temple courts, surrounded by the teachers of the Law. Jesus was attentive to them, responding and asking questions of them as well. One of the most interesting aspects of this entire situation is the way in which both Jesus' questions and responses impressed the teachers. Note the text says "...*all who heard Jesus were astonished at his understanding and his answers.*" We get the unmistakable impression that not only was Jesus intelligent, but He was way beyond His years in wisdom and understanding when it came to God's Word.

First, the wisdom that Jesus possessed certainly came from the fact that He was God, but as He was also fully human, it necessitated study on his part. Though He was fully God, He was still required to do what all of us human beings do, and that is to study God's Word. It did not come via osmosis. He did not go to sleep with the scrolls under his head, thinking that throughout the night, His brain would absorb the information. Our Lord applied Himself to the effort of reading, studying and learning the Word of God, which sounds odd since He was and remains *the* Word of God.

Does this section of Scripture tell us anything about debating? Not directly. It merely points out that His wisdom impressed those who were much older than He was and who had more years of studying under their belts. Verse 52 of this same chapter informs us "...*Jesus increased in wisdom and in stature, and in favor with God and with people.*" Again, this did not occur because Jesus was (and remains) fully God. Being fully God put Him in the position of *not* being able to sin. Being fully human put Him in the position of being able not to sin. He needed to grow, to mature, and to study to show Himself approved just as we are to do. There is no better model than Jesus.

It is tempting to think of Jesus as One who went through life never being able to sin, and therefore never really having to deal with the pressures of temptation. Yet the writer of Hebrews tells us that the exact opposite existed. *"During his earthly life Christ offered both requests and supplications, with loud cries and tears, to the one who was able to save him from death and he was heard because of his devotion. Although he was a son, he learned obedience through the things he suffered. And by being perfected in this way, he became the source of eternal salvation to all who obey him, and he was designated by God as high priest in the order of Melchizedek,"* (Hebrews 5:7-10). This is not just referring to the situation in the Garden of Gethsemane, which may immediately come to mind, the night He was betrayed. The text specifically states *"during His earthly life..."* Every step along the way, He dealt with the pressures of some type of temptation. These temptations, though He never once gave into any of them, were allowed, to *"perfect"* Him. This word "perfect" does not mean that He was *imperfect* before. It means it *completed* Him through the teaching that each situation provided and in learning to lean not on His own strength, but strength from above.

Because Jesus was literally put through the test as we are, He can and does relate to our weaknesses. *"For we do not have a high priest incapable of sympathizing with our weaknesses, but one who has been tempted in every way just as we are, yet without sin,"* (Hebrews 4:15).

Therefore, in the Temple scenario, it is clear that Jesus was way ahead of the crowd in wisdom and understanding. Yet, at the same time, it is also clear that He *listened* to their instruction as well. This is the mark of a wise individual. They are secure and able to listen to the wisdom that others have within.

We find another situation with Jesus, just prior to the beginning of His public ministry, in which He faces His greatest adversary, Satan. In this situation, the enemy of our souls, attempted to cause Jesus to sin. Had He stumbled here, He would have sinned. If He *had* sinned, He would have immediately been preempted from continuing, and would have lost the ability to act as the perfect propitiation for us, on our behalf.

In Luke 4, we read of this encounter with Satan. It is an interestingly diabolical time in Christ's life that we are privy to, and if understood correctly, allows us to see just how important two things are:

1. The truth of God's Word
2. Understanding the truth of God's Word

In other words, many people read the Bible, and believe they understand it. This is not necessarily the case though. We know that every founder of every cult has read at least parts of the Bible, yet believes it to say something that it does not say. We have people who believe the Bible teaches that God is *one*, not three in one. They believe that at times, He represented Himself as the Father, while at other times, as the Son, and still other times, as the Holy Spirit. In all those cases, they believe that He was always and only one Being at one time. These folks disallow the Trinity.

Some believe that Jesus was the first created Being, *never* God, but that He *became* divine by being "born of the Spirit," and emanating from the Father. Some believe that Jesus was merely a Christ "consciousness," and that anyone can become that very same thing.

Mormons believe they are in fact, the only authentic Christians. Others, like the Jehovah's Witnesses, believe unique things that are wholly unorthodox. The trouble is that simply *reading* the Bible (while this needs to be done), is only the first step. A determined understanding of how best to interpret the Bible is also necessary, so that pitfalls of false interpretations are avoided.

If we consider Christ's encounter with Satan, we realize very quickly that Satan knew (and knows), God's Word backwards and forwards. He understands nuances of it better than anyone alive (except Jesus). It is because of this and his extreme intelligence, that he has the ability to twist Scripture, causing us to think it means one thing, when it can literally mean something else.

Note the first temptation of Christ. Jesus has been in the wilderness for forty days and Luke tells us that He had eaten nothing. He was very hungry. Knowing this, the Tempter comes along with this suggestion in Luke 4:3, "*If you are the Son of God, command this stone to become bread.*" Satan knew of course that Jesus was extremely hungry. Go ahead and make some bread for yourself, he suggested to Jesus. Christ refused and stated, "*Man does not live by bread alone.*" Satan was not even that subtle here, because he completely underestimated Jesus.

For us, the suggestion might have been (if we were in the same situation), "*Hey, head over across the street to that market and take a loaf of bread, since you have no money. You are going to die of hunger if you don't eat! Surely, God will understand.*" Either way you cut it, that is stealing and something God would not want us to do, so then our response should be "*The Bible says, 'Do not steal'.*"

In the next round, Satan takes a harder approach. However, it is still obvious. He is offering a proposition to Christ. Jesus should worship him (Satan), and all the kingdoms of the world would be given to Christ in exchange. Again, Jesus quotes from the Bible by stating, "*You are to worship the Lord your God and serve only him.*" So far, each time, Jesus met Satan head on with the active, living Word of God.

Okay, Satan thinks. If Jesus wants to play the quote-the-Bible game, two can play. Therefore, he hits him with something directly from Scripture in the third round of this spiritual boxing match. After suggesting that He jump off from the high point of the Temple, Satan reasons, "*it is written, 'He will command his angels concerning you, to protect you,' and 'with their hands they will lift you up, so that you will not strike your foot against a stone'.*" Here, Satan tries his hand at quoting Scripture, applying it to a situation; however, he has twisted it to mean something it does not mean. Christ immediately saw through it and responded with, "*You are not to put the Lord your God to the test.*"

After this third try, Satan left Jesus in defeat...for a time. The point is that Jesus did not enter into debate with Satan. He simply presented the truth of God's Word and let that speak to the situation. No debate was required, but merely a presentation of applicable truth and Satan is defeated. If Jesus needed to do that, how much more do *we* need to do that? However, it is equally important to realize that simply knowing Scripture is not enough. Knowing *which* Scripture applies to *which* situation is where the rubber actually meets the road.

In these and other situations, **Jesus *never* debated. He stated**.

One of the next big tests of Christ's mettle occurred shortly after His public baptism following the temptation in the wilderness. In Luke 4, after these two events, we read of the beginning of Jesus' public ministry. He returned to Galilee, after enduring the testing by Satan, and we read, "*Jesus, in the power of the Spirit, returned to Galilee, and news about him spread throughout the surrounding countryside. He began to teach in their synagogues and was praised by all,*" (Luke 4:14-150. After His first major battle (and win), with Satan, and public baptism, Jesus officially entered public ministry. At that point, everyone liked what he or she heard from Him. They were amazed. They praised Him, undoubtedly because of His wisdom. The Bible does not tell us what He said at this point, but that he simply "began to teach" and His Word was received remarkably well. What happens next however, is the exact opposite of this.

Chapter 9

Refusing the Truth

BUT IT'S TRUE! JESUS LOVES YOU AND HE DIED SO THAT YOU MIGHT HAVE ETERNAL LIFE!

DUDE...TALK TO THE HAND! GOT NO TIME FOR FAIRY TALES!

©2009 F. DERUVO

The Bible tells us that Jesus next headed to the town of Nazareth. It was here that Jesus encountered His first real problem. Luke tells us *"Now Jesus came to Nazareth, where he had been brought up, and went into the synagogue on the Sabbath day, as was his custom. He stood up to read, and the scroll of the prophet Isaiah was given to him,"* (Luke 4:16-17). Jesus arrives to Nazareth, where He had been raised as a boy, and went into the synagogue as He normally did. This time, someone handed Him the scroll of Isaiah. This would not have been an uncommon practice. Jesus was now a man, having reached the age of thirty. The leaders of that particular synagogue gave Him the honor of reading from God's Word publicly. Jesus accepted the invitation, and He reads the following words:

> "The Spirit of the Lord is upon me, because he has anointed me to proclaim good news to the poor. He has sent me to proclaim release to the captives and the regaining of sight to the blind, to set free those who are oppressed, to proclaim the year of the Lord's favor," (Luke 4:18-20).

Jesus quoted Isaiah 61:1-2a, but did not finish the entire verse from that passage. Chuck Missler comments on this, stating, "*Where Jesus stopped reading is significant. In the text of Isaiah there is a comma where he chose to finish (verse 2). The part of the text Jesus did not include is, 'and the day of the vengeance of our God.' He read the part of the mandate that He would fulfill in his first appearance. Yet to be fulfilled is, 'the day of vengeance of our God,' which will be at His Second Coming.*"[2]

Luke then tells us that Jesus finished reading, rolled up the scroll, gave it back to the synagogue attendant, and sat down. We learn that everyone in the place just stared at him. Jesus responds to their stares with the words, "*Today this scripture has been fulfilled even as you heard it being read,*" (Luke 4:21). Luke tells us that even though they spoke "well of Him," they began questioning His credentials, by pointing to His pedigree, saying, "*Isn't this Joseph's son?*" (cf. 4:22b) Though Luke does not indicate that all of the people present were asking this, it is possible that while some thought well of Him, others – possibly leaders of the synagogue – began immediately criticizing the fact that His father

---

[2] Chuck Missler, *Learn the Bible in 24 Hours* (Nashville: Thomas Nelson 2002), 128

was Joseph. There was a tendency to believe that Jesus was an illegitimate son, by a woman who had gotten pregnant out of wedlock. Though never proven, it had undoubtedly been discussed. Even if it had not been discussed, what was difficult for some to believe is that this individual could be the "chosen One" since they had seen Him grow up as a boy among them.   How could He be the Messiah, if we saw him as a baby and young boy? They were expecting the Messiah to just appear one day out of the blue, having never seen Him or heard of Him. Since they knew Jesus' parents and lineage, that ruled out the possibility of His being the actual Messiah. The idiom, *familiarity breeds contempt*, is certainly true in this instance. The people were familiar with Jesus and His upbringing as a child among them.

Jesus' response to them is telling. Rather than attempt to prove that He was in fact, who He claimed to be, he simply rebuked them through a prophesy regarding the situation, which found fulfillment on the day He died, (cf. Luke 4:23-24). Jesus then pointed out a few things that these Jewish worshipers did not want to hear. In verses 25 to 30 of Luke 4, Jesus states,

> *"But in truth I tell you, there were many widows in Israel in Elijah's days, when the sky was shut up three and a half years, and there was a great famine over all the land. Yet Elijah was sent to none of them, but only to a woman who was a widow at Zarephath in Sidon. And there were many lepers in Israel in the time of the prophet Elisha, yet none of them was cleansed except Naaman the Syrian."When they heard this, all the people in the synagogue were filled with rage. They got up, forced him out of the town, and brought him to the brow of the hill on which their town was built, so that they could throw him down the cliff. But he passed through the crowd and went on his way."*

The tragedy of the above section of Scripture is threefold:

1. Jesus reminded the Jewish worshipers that because of the severe iniquity in Israel during the days of Elijah, God passed over all of the Jewish widows to help a *Gentile* widow at Zarephath. This same situation existed with Elisha, with God bypassing all the Jewish lepers, to help a leper who was *Gentile*.
2. Though He spoke the Truth, Jesus' listeners rejected that Truth simply because it made them *angry*.
3. Their anger, which stemmed from pricked consciences, resulted in wanting *and* attempting to kill the Messenger.

Notice though, that in none of this, did Jesus attempt to convince His hearers of anything. He simply stated the truth and let the chips fall where they would fall. In this case, the truth was so unwelcome that it caused them to seek His death.

Again, we are not privy to know who, or how many of the people in the synagogue that morning actually wanted to kill, or did participate in attempting to kill Jesus. We know that as far as Luke was concerned, it seemed to be the whole assembly, so it was probably more than simply a couple of individuals. It would seem that a good majority of them all decided that the best thing that could happen to this Jesus was to see if He could fly. Note the text says that Jesus simply passed through, or disappeared from the crowd. That must have confused them, but it did not change their minds about Him.

This is the fascinating thing, not only about Jesus, but also about the Bible. Jesus never caved into those who insisted that He prove His authority. The Bible itself never caves into those who insist that God must prove His existence. The Bible simply *assumes* God's existence. It makes no attempt to prove it, which makes sense since God wrote it. We either accept that, or we reject it, but God makes no effort to prove what Paul says in the first chapter of Romans all people already know the truth to be. The proof of God's existence is seen in His handiwork, the Creation. Though evolutionists have attempted to preempt, subvert, and suppress the knowledge of God through His Creation, they have only succeeded in providing fodder to those who do not *want* to believe that God exists.

Not long ago, I spoke with an atheist who told me that it is easy to prove that God does not exist. What he means of course, is that it is easy for him to *believe* that God does not exist. He has gotten to that point solely because he fought against God enough in the futility of his thinking, so God gave him over to a depraved mind (cf. Romans 1). He would disagree, saying he can prove God does not exist. There we go again, back to the arena of debate.

Neither the Bible, nor Jesus Christ, nor the Holy Spirit, nor the Father need to prove anything to anyone. Yet, humanity continues to bark their orders to God, as if He must kowtow and jump to our commands.

Therefore, in this instance, we see that Jesus did not debate with these individuals. He did not attempt to convince them of the meaning of the Isaiah passage. He did not try to make His Words plainer to them. Like Ezekiel of old, who was told that he was to say to the house of Israel what God told him to say – *whether or not they listened* – so also did Jesus do the same thing, *whether or not they listened*.

This is an extremely important concept for Christians to grasp. Our job as Christians is to do the will of Him who saves and then sends us. We are *not* responsible for the outcome. We are only responsible for our words and actions, ensuring that they are what God wants us to say and do. Yes, there are times when we will be on the receiving end of ridicule, ire, vitriol and anger, but this should in no way stop us from completing God's will. We will answer to God when we face Him, not the person who reeks with disdain for us because of what we say, based on what we believe.

For Jesus, life went on, He continued with His ministry, and it is not until nearly the end of the fifth chapter of Luke that He runs up against the hard-heartedness and legality of the Pharisees. By the time we arrive at this section of Scriptures, Jesus has called disciples, healed a leprous man, healed and *forgave* a paralytic, called Levi (Matthew), and ate with "sinners."

Because Matthew was so grateful for his newfound faith, he put on a banquet for Jesus. All of Matthew's tax collecting friends attended, and as you can imagine, the Pharisees and teachers of the Law were not happy about it. Interestingly enough though, according to Luke, they did not dare approach Jesus with their complaint, but went instead to Jesus' disciples (as if they would know). I am sure they figured that they would be able to lord it over those generally unlearned men, whom Jesus had called to be His disciples.

"But the Pharisees and their experts in the law complained to his disciples, saying, 'Why do you eat and drink with tax collectors and sinners?' Jesus answered them, 'Those who are well don't need a physician, but those who are sick do. I have not come to call the righteous, but sinners to repentance'," (Luke 5:30-32).

If you will look at the above Scripture passage, note that even though the Pharisees and "lawyers" bypassed Jesus with their concerns, Jesus responded to their query. Ouch. The Temple legalists must not have liked that much. Here they thought they could arm-wrestle the disciples into submission, but when facing Jesus Himself, they were at a decided disadvantage. They should have quit while they were ahead, but chose to muscle on anyway, by claiming, *"John's disciples frequently fast and pray, and so do the disciples of the Pharisees, but yours continue to eat and drink,"* (Luke 5:33). In verse 34, we read Jesus' response, *"You cannot make the wedding guests fast while the bridegroom is with them, can you? But those days are coming, and when the bridegroom is taken from them, at that time they will fast."*

The Pharisees and legalists tried to turn the attention *from* Jesus *to* His disciples (using the example of John's disciples), but Jesus would have none of it, pointing the finger right back to Himself. He was well aware of the fact that the Pharisees were really questioning Him, and His actions, not the actions of His disciples. They were too hypocritical to admit that though, so Jesus responded with an answer that directed the attention back to Him, where it belonged. At the same time, His response said to them that He was aware of their word play and He was not going to be taken in by it.

Please note though, that Jesus is not debating them at this point. He is making statements that they are free either to accept or to reject. Ultimately, they chose to *reject* every step of the way. During the entirety of His public ministry, nothing Jesus did or said convinced them of their error.

The next chapter in Luke's narrative again pits Israel's religious leaders against the Lord of glory and once again, they lose. This is the section where Jesus is going through the fields and helping Himself to some of the leftover grain. Though this was permissible under the Mosaic Law, the Pharisees had a problem with it because Jesus was doing this on a Sabbath. He was being accused of "working," and the Law forbade that. Here is the text in Luke 6:1-5 (NET):

Jesus was going through the grain fields on a Sabbath, and his disciples picked some heads of wheat, rubbed them in their hands, and ate them. But some of the Pharisees said, 'Why are you doing what is against the law on the Sabbath?' Jesus answered them, 'Haven't you read what David did when he and his companions were hungry —how he entered the house of God, took and ate the sacred bread, which is not lawful for any to eat but the priests alone, and gave it to his companions?' Then he said to them, 'The Son of Man is lord of the Sabbath'."

The Pharisees were far from happy here, about what Jesus and His disciples were doing. It looked like a good debate was on the horizon. Since the Pharisees were relying on the Law, they believed they had their end of the debate covered. They had caught Jesus in an unmistakable faux pas, which was actually *sin,* and they were happy to accuse Him of it.

Jesus, on the other hand, was well acquainted with the Law that they were referring to, which is recorded for us in Deuteronomy 23:25: *"When you go into the ripe grain fields of your neighbor you may pluck off the kernels with your hand, but you must not use a sickle on your neighbor's ripe grain."*

To the Pharisees, what Jesus and His disciples did was illegal, according to the Mosaic Law. There was to be no work. What they were doing constituted work by the very fact that they had to walk through the field, plucking the heads of grain and rolling it in their hands. This separated the outer covering from the kernel. It did not matter to the Pharisees that the disciples had not eaten since the day prior (cf. Matthew 12:1; Mark 2:23). What mattered to them was the very letter of the Law, and it was certainly not being upheld by Christ at that point! They had something to say about that.

While the Pharisees argue that this was unlawful, Jesus makes the astounding statement that He (the Son of Man) "is lord of the Sabbath." What a strange thing to say indeed! What could He possibly mean? Well, for one thing, this statement is a nod to His deity. He is affirming the fact that He is Lord over the Sabbath! Note that Christ used the example of David eating the showbread found within the Temple (cf. Luke 6:4; 1 Samuel 21:1-6). In effect, Jesus was saying that He was far greater than David was and that comment would not have been missed by these Pharisees. What they *had* missed was the fact that the Mosaic Law, which included the commandment to keep the Sabbath holy by avoiding work, was not to be misconstrued to say that people should not be able to feed themselves on that day. Since both Jesus and the disciples were hungry, then they simply stopped to do what law allowed, taking some of the grain that was left in the field. This was *not* work, because eating was not considered *work*.

In fact, it is likely that these same Pharisees had eaten that day, and they had to lift food to their mouths to do it. They may have even had to ladle food from a pot to a bowl. Nonetheless, unless someone else fed them, they fed themselves and in the process, had done the same thing that Jesus and His disciples were now doing. Talk about hypocrisy.

However, Christ again does not seek to debate with them. His questions are rhetorical in nature, designed to display the obviousness of the unstated response. He pointedly asked them, *"Haven't you read what David did when he and his companions were hungry – how he entered the house of God, took and ate the sacred bread, which is not lawful for any to eat but the priests alone, and gave it to his companions?"* (6:3b-4). Jesus was not expecting an answer, and certainly they had none to provide. By asking a question, He was not inviting them to debate Him. Certainly, they could have attempted to do so, but they realized when they were beaten and left it at that.

In many ways, the Pharisees are symbolic of our own adversary, the devil. Satan works to trip us up at any cost, and the only thing that stops him is Truth and the only place that Truth is found is in God's Word.

Chapter 10

Apologetics or Debate?

T here is a huge difference between *presenting* an appropriate apologetic, and debating an issue. The former seeks to instruct and even correct, while the latter normally veers off into endless argumentation. It is imperative to know when to instruct and when to *stop* instructing. Of course, we often continue, "discussing" with someone when we should have stopped a while ago. This serves no purpose really. We can probably all remember times when we continued hammering a point home only to create a rift between the individual and ourselves.

In truth, it is sometimes a fine line between instructing and debating, so it takes a sensitive, loving heart *for* the plight of the other person, and sensitivity to the leading of the Holy Spirit as well. Sometimes, a few well-chosen words can do more good than an hour-long discussion, which turns into a debate.

Most people come by their religious views the same way they come by their political or sports views. They grow up with them. This does not mean they never change those viewpoints, but initially, if someone is raised in an atheistic household, they will tend to carry on that tradition. Someone who is born into a home where one particular professional sports team has been the norm for decades will likely grow to embrace that same sports team. Again, things do not always necessarily remain this way, but they often start out this way.

The same holds true for politics. People normally continue to uphold the political traditions of the home in which they were raised. If you have ever gotten into a political discussion with someone who is of the opposite party, you know how quickly things can get ugly. Why is this so? Simply because people usually hold opinions close to their heart, and those strong opinions are attached to their emotions. It is ridiculous to think that by pointing out what you consider wrong with their candidate, they are immediately going to respond with something like, *"Wow, I am so glad you pointed that out! I never noticed that before you said anything. I am withdrawing my support immediately."* Not only is that response far-fetched, but in today's society, anyone who made a statement like that would likely be in sarcastic mode.

Even though most adopt their viewpoints as they grow up, there comes a point when people normally either fully embrace those opinions as theirs, or they reject them for another. Most do not do this lightly.

In the most recent presidential election, I was amazed to see how many people thought that our current president was "the hope" of the masses and once he became president, then things would change for the better. I was not at all convinced of that fact. Certainly, because I was not a member of that political party, that alone kept me from embracing his platform somewhat. However, other things also prompted me to reject him out of hand, like his voting record on abortion, as well as his seeming unwillingness to say whether he was a Christian or Muslim. I had my suspicions, but wanted to hear him say it. Maybe he did not want to alienate anyone, by allowing people to pigeonhole him. In either case, my judgment was telling me that Barack Obama was not the best candidate for the United States. I simply stayed away from the debate because of how heated things were becoming. Now that President Obama is our current president, then my job – according to Scripture – is to pray for him, that God will use him for His purposes. I firmly believe God will do just that.

People become upset and argumentative over many areas of life. Discussing it does not often help because people feel so strongly about these particular issues. So what do we do, never discuss it? Not at all. We should feel free to discuss it, but we should never feel free to

- Shove our opinions down someone else's throat
- Debate them until they cry "uncle!"

As Christians, we must express our opinion with tact, charity, and brevity. In the first chapter of this book, I referenced a situation in which a number of us in seminary got into a heated debate over an issue, the subject of which I do not even remember. Even though the nature of the issue escapes memory, one thing does not. I recall one of the guys was unflappable when he shared his opinion. Looking back now, I believe that his opinion then was right on and mine was incorrect. He simply did not become ruffled though when a number of us verbally ganged up on him. He was sure in his opinion; that it was based solidly

Hate Under Pressure?

OR
Grace Under Pressure?

on Scripture and he needed no one to agree with him about it. He rested on what he understood as the truth of God's Word.

There was an issue, which was constantly being bandied about in the news in those days. Since we were right next to Philadelphia, which was home to a number of television studios, the seminary was called upon from time to time when a TV talk show was dealing with a subject of a religious nature.

This same person from our TV lounge room debate volunteered to be part of the live audience when a station called for volunteers. When asked about it later, he indicated that during the show he *was* called on to provide his opinion. After providing it, was soundly *booed* by many within the audience, but maintained a calm that comes from knowing that you possess the truth. That is grace under pressure and that is what Christians need to exercise more of today.

Often, debates are not so obvious as a TV talk show scenario. Some within the visible Church are almost sneaky about their intent or desire to debate another person. It is almost as if they want to wine and dine you into the debate by being winsome and cheerful. Then, before you know it, you are embroiled in a full-on debate that often times becomes so muddled and confused, that most of the time is spent simply defining terminology!

Not long ago, I joined a forum strictly because of the statement of faith. I agreed with and assumed (bad mistake), that all who participated in discussion (I will call it that for now), agreed with it as well. It did not take long to realize that people continue to come to these forums for the sole purpose of kicking up dust.

One day, I went into one of the threads and saw this post:

> *"Hi Fred; I was just going over some articles on your web site; and intend to return and peruse the topics there*

having to do with apostate trends; in hope that I will be brought up to date on the curiosities that are arising like mushrooms [or is it toadstools?] in some religious circles. I noticed in one article on eschatology that you maintain that pre-trib was taught in the early Church. Can you provide any quotes from the early centuries that support that position? It is known that premillennialism was the original position held to in the early Church; however that fact does not necessarily prove that pre-trib doctrine was taught there."

Immediately a red flag went off in my mind, because here was an intelligent-*sounding* individual, who was apparently trying to pretend that he was actually interested in reading any support I might have for my position. It was apparent, once I read past his congenial verbiage, that agreeing with me was the furthest thing from his mind. He continued,

"Many quotes from the early centuries concerning the end time tribulation period reveal that Christians expected the Church to be subject to a time of persecution under the man of sin; which facts rule against the distinctive precepts found within pre-trib doctrine. I have not been able to find any evidence to the effect that pre-trib was taught in the early Church; which tends to support the position that pre-trib is of rather recent origin; such having arose in about the 1830's; in England. The doctrine attributed to J.N. Darby is found to have immediately preceded him; howbeit in a 'partial rapturist' form; and that prior to his having espoused his dispensationalist 'two stage return of the Lord' variant."

Finishing his post brought two things immediately to light:

1. I became immediately aware that he was fishing, attempting to draw me into a debate, and
2. He apparently believed I was unable to see through his surreptitious approach

My response consisted of, *"Let's cut to the chase - you're not a PreTrib Rapturist, so you want to attempt to prove that I'm wrong. I have no interest in debating with you at all; you or anyone else."*

Unfortunately, like any person whose sole intent is to debate in order to prove a point, he persisted. We went back and forth a number of times and at one point, one of the moderators came into the thread and offered a gentle rebuke to this verbal adversary. It did no good at all, so I tried again to impress upon him my complete lack of desire to debate, but that made no difference. By this time, another individual had also gotten involved in the same debate. I noticed that she had arrived to the board a mere few days prior to the other person, and now they were filling up the threads with their own conversations, giving each other enough 'high fives' to make you think you were at a professional ball game. The tag-teaming was a bit much.

Interestingly enough, nothing either of these two said agreed with the *statement of faith* of the board, yet they barreled along, purposefully oblivious to those beliefs. They apparently believed that presenting a demeanor, which reeked in pseudo-politeness (or bullishness), would nullify the fact that they were simply on the opposite side of the theological fence as everyone else.

My position was again reiterated regarding my complete lack of desire to *debate*. That was met by this response, *"For a man given to scholarly studies I find it ironic that you would in essence say that you don't want to discuss scripture with anyone who does not agree with your interpretation of such..."*

I am sure you see what he was attempting to do at this point. My response was, *"It is easy to see why you have such erroneous biblical viewpoints when you make the mistake of believing that the words DEBATE and DISCUSS are interchangeable. In spite of your pseudo-intellectual presentation, it is clear that the nuances of the language escape you."*

We had essentially stopped discussing anything theological and had begun the process of debating, in the form of one-liners and ad hominem attacks. He called into question the true nature of my scholarship, and I in turn, questioned his ability to understand the English language. It had become childish and *that*, my friends is the problem when anything like discussion turns to debate. He was becoming more aggressive in his comments, while I did what I could to avoid him.

You might be glad to know that in short order, the thread was locked and the two individuals in question were barred from further posting. Now the sad part is that these two people are entitled to their opinions, but to deliberately go to a forum that supports and espouses opinions which are in opposition to theirs is fruitless. Do folks like this really think they are going to win friends and converts? I have *never* seen it happen, due solely to the fact that people who go to forums to begin with, normally already know what they believe and why they believe it.

This is true of debating. No one gets into a debate unless he believes he has something to *say*, and that he is *right* about it. No one debates in order to *learn* something. That is called *instruction*, or *discussion*. Folks debate in order to *win* something; namely, the debate itself.

I would like to stress though, that not all debate is bad, nor does it always end up in a mudslinging contest. There have been many academic debates held within educational halls and auditoriums throughout the world, which have been *beneficial*, if for no other reason than the fact that they were civil and even pleasant to listen to as both sides presented their views. In fact, I have a number of these educational debates on DVD, which I watch from time to time. I watch them to see if I can determine when or where an individual failed to answer a direct question, or got off on some other tangent.

One I watched online for the first time recently was between Frank Turek, co-author of *I Don't Have Enough Faith to be an Atheist*, and Christopher Hitchens, author of *god is not Great: How Religion Poisons Everything*.

What was particularly enjoyable was that the two men obviously seemed to respect one another. What was frustrating about it was listening to Hitchens' meanderings. It was almost as if he gave absolutely no thought to his answer, but simply opened his mouth and words came out. The words in at least some cases, did not even directly respond to a query posed by Turek or the audience. He often injected humor and asides in his responses as well. This is not bad at all, however, it would have helped had he thoroughly answered the questions.

Now, do I believe anyone changed his or her beliefs by the time the debate had concluded? I do not think so however, I could be wrong. Certainly, there was little in the way of new information in the debate from either party that caused me to respond with wide-eyed curiosity or interest. It was an hour and a half of listening to the same type of thing most of us have heard on many occasions and in a variety of ways. It was not awful and because of the lively and confident demeanor of both men, the hour and a half passed fairly quickly. It was apparent both men were well versed in why they believed what they believe and in the end that is all that can be asked.

The reality of changing someone's opinion after listening to a debate is low simply because many people today have strong opinions on what they believe. They may not be able to accurately express why their belief system is the more logical, but for them, they are satisfied.

In a way then, debates are a type of Victorian era type of duel. There are all the proper accoutrements, including respect (and possibly even praise), for one's opponent, a solid understanding of the subject to be debated, along with a level of comfort in public speaking. It is entertainment in the truest sense of the word. Instead of watching two men pummel each other with fisticuffs, verbiage is utilized to strike a blow.

Again, it cannot be emphasized enough that every Christian *must* know what they believe and why they believe it. They must also be prepared to give everyone an answer for the hope that they possess in Christ. Nowhere in Scripture (that I can find), are we told to debate others who have differing viewpoints. We are told to *instruct* and *teach*, but we cannot be held responsible for anyone's reaction to our instruction. They may well choose to reject it and if they do, we are not responsible for that. If they accept it, we are also not responsible for that because that is a work of God through the Holy Spirit.

This is patently clear from Paul's (as well as Jesus'), interactions with many people throughout the book of Acts. He often attempted to debate them, by trying to convince them that they were wrong and what he offered them – eternal life through Jesus Christ – was the only way to God. This often failed and Paul was not an idiot. He was extremely well trained and had tremendous schooling, yet some in the book of Acts did not respect his learning and thought he was someone just mouthing off, with no real understanding to back up his claims.

We must teach and instruct. We must be willing to be a mouthpiece for God and to go where He would have us go. We must do our part and leave God's part to God.

Chapter 11

The Master's Example

On many occasions, Jesus could have easily gotten caught up in arguing, but He did not allow that. He stated the Truth and let the chips fall where they may. He was not intent on persuading or debating subjects to death. He knew that served no purpose at all, and was much more counter-productive than anything else was.

We last saw Jesus in chapter six of Luke, when the Pharisees were hounding Him about "working" on the Sabbath, in spite of the fact that nothing He was doing was illegal, either by Roman standards, or by way of the Mosaic Law.   The absurdity of the Pharisees' outlook and attitude is clearly seen in the next situation that Luke reports. Beginning with verse six of chapter six, Luke tells us of another Sabbath, in which Jesus chose to heal someone who had a withered hand.

The text states, *"On another Sabbath, Jesus entered the synagogue and was teaching. Now a man was there whose right hand was withered. The experts in the law and the Pharisees watched Jesus closely to see if he would heal on the Sabbath, so that they could find a reason to accuse him. But he knew their thoughts, and said to the man who had the withered hand, 'Get up and stand here.' So he rose and stood there. Then Jesus said to them, 'I ask you, is it lawful to do good on the Sabbath or to do evil, to save a life or to destroy it?' After looking around at them all, he said to the man, 'Stretch out your hand.' The man did so, and his hand was restored. But they were filled with mindless rage and began debating with one another what they would do to Jesus,"* (Luke 6:6-11, NET).

Here is one situation where Jesus is deliberately drawing the Pharisees and the experts of the Law out. He pointedly asks them a question, which is designed to show them the shallowness of their own hearts. Interestingly enough, the reason He is said to have asked this question is that he "knew their thoughts." They were all looking intently at Him to see whether Jesus would heal the man.

How ironic this entire situation truly is, where the Pharisees are concerned. They apparently knew that Jesus *could* heal, and instead of being excited or grateful for that, they were suspicious and resentful. Why? Because to them at least, Jesus was not the *type* of Messiah they were expecting to see. They wanted someone who would ride in on a proverbial white horse, and overthrow the Roman power, thereby freeing Israel from that tyranny once and for all. The type of Messiah they were expecting would be fierce in countenance and powerful, one that would not put up with the unfairness that was constantly being committed against Jewish people and Israel herself. They did not want some namby-pamby do-gooding Messiah, who only thought about healing the sick and feeding the hungry! What about the Roman Empire's domination of Israel and the Jewish people? To the Pharisees, Jesus was a wimp, concerned more about the welfare of individual people than of the overall nation of Israel. No one with such a soft heart would ever have a chance of defeating Rome!

So it was at every chance, they tore into Jesus, and their fear of Him made it that much more treacherous. In fact, because of the stubbornness of their hearts, the Pharisees decided immediately after Jesus healed the paralytic that they definitely needed to do something about Him. Luke reports that they were "filled with mindless rage" which caused them to begin "debating with one another about what they would do with Jesus." Mindless rage tells us all we need to know. These Pharisees were no more interested in hearing and facing the truth than they were of allowing Jesus to live. He had become a threat to them. He was threatening their very existence and role in society. While they had no supernatural power over Him, they felt certain they could kill Him, and so they began to plan. Jesus however, continued to minister. Though the Pharisees debated about what they should do with Jesus, Jesus never entered that debate. He knew that His life was in the palm of His Father's hand. He also knew that His life would take leave of His mortal body when He gave the gave His spirit into the Father's hands.

As Jesus continued to minister throughout the region of Galilee, his fame continued to go before Him. Wherever He went, He loved people and He showed this love by what He did for them. Whether He fed them, preached to them, or healed them, He did all of it because of His deep love and affection for them. He wanted them to have a Good Shepherd, not like the Pharisees and Scribes, who were in the ministry for themselves. They loved being the talk of the town, and loved it when people moved out of their way as they walked through the town square or market place. They loved the adoration and the praise. In fact, they actually believed they were as good as the people told them they were, but in truth, they were far from it. However, the accolades, the position, the respect and reverence they received consistently blinded them to the fact that they were heartless, evil, and nothing even close to what God considered a good shepherd. They were miserable failures, and Jesus' very presence, teaching, and healings pointed this out to them every day.

Therefore, it is not surprising that at least one of the Pharisees opted to invite Jesus over for dinner. We read about this beginning in Luke 7:36 and following.

> "Now one of the Pharisees asked Jesus to have dinner with him, so he went into the Pharisee's house and took his place at the table. Then when a woman of that town, who was a sinner, learned that Jesus was dining at the Pharisee's house, she brought an alabaster jar of perfumed oil. As she stood behind him at his feet, weeping, she began to wet his feet with her tears. She wiped them with her hair, kissed them, and anointed them with the perfumed oil. Now when the Pharisee who had invited him saw this, he said to himself, 'If this man were a prophet, he would know who and what kind of woman this is who is touching him, that she is a sinner.' So Jesus answered him, 'Simon, I have something to say to you.' He replied, 'Say it, Teacher.' 'A certain creditor had two debtors; one owed him five hundred silver coins, and the other fifty. When they could not pay, he canceled the debts of both. Now which of them will love him more?' Simon answered, 'I suppose the one who had the bigger debt canceled.' Jesus

*said to him, 'You have judged rightly.' Then, turning
toward the woman, he said to Simon, 'Do you see this
woman? I entered your house. You gave me no water for
my feet, but she has wet my feet with her tears and wiped
them with her hair. You gave me no kiss of greeting, but
from the time I entered she has not stopped kissing my
feet. You did not anoint my head with oil, but she has
anointed my feet with perfumed oil. Therefore I tell you,
her sins, which were many, are forgiven, thus she loved
much; but the one who is forgiven little loves little.' Then
Jesus said to her, 'Your sins are forgiven.' But those who
were at the table with him began to say among
themselves, 'Who is this, who even forgives sins?' He said
to the woman, 'Your faith has saved you; go in peace'."*
(Luke 7:36-50, NET).

There are a number of things happening in this passage of Scripture, but please note that not once does Jesus enter into a debate with this Pharisee. Jesus merely makes clear statements of truth, which cut Simon to the quick. However, instead of recognizing that Jesus was indeed, a "prophet" of the highest order, Simon rejects that truth. He failed to repent, which biblically means to change one's mind about Christ. After being presented with *the* truth, Simon's anger toward Jesus grows.

Let us consider the situation. First, Simon invites Jesus to his home for dinner. During the course of the evening, a woman comes in. She is no ordinary woman, but a "sinner." In an act of pure and wholesome love for Jesus, she opens an expensive bottle of perfume and anoints Jesus' feet with it. Her tears stream down from her eyes and mix with the perfume as she wipes Jesus' feet with her own hair. What an act of servitude she displayed here.

Can you imagine for a moment, just how *indignant* and *incensed* Simon became, as he sat there, watching this strange scene unfold before him? How *dare* this woman enter into *his* home, and fawn over this Jesus! How on *earth* could Jesus allow this to continue?

Luke tells us that this woman was a "sinner" and that could mean anything, but more than likely, it was a decent way of saying that she was a prostitute. Simon is more concerned about the fact that Jesus should know who this woman is ('*if He was really a prophet*'), than the fact that she is in his house to begin with, thereby making it *unclean*. His inner reaction and hidden thoughts are not hidden to Jesus.

You have to appreciate the next part. Jesus says he wants to tell Simon something, and Simon responds with "Say it, Teacher." If ever there was a patronizing response, this was it. Simon probably had to grit his teeth when he called Jesus "teacher." Oh what an awful taste that must have left in his mouth! Nonetheless, Jesus tells him a simple story and he likely made it unmistakably simple, so that Simon would have no problem grasping the point. In fact, it was embarrassingly simple and pointedly so.

The point of the story is beautifully illustrated. The woman – a "sinner" – showed more love for Jesus than Simon would ever even consider showing to Him. In fact, Simon never even offered the normal social considerations to Jesus, such as having water handy so that Jesus could wash His own feet prior to entering Simon's home. The entire evening's dinner had been a charade, designed by Simon and his cronies to find out what they could find out about Jesus, by pretending to respect Him.

Another clear point of Jesus' illustration is that Simon likely thought himself to be spiritually perfect, or complete, lacking nothing. He would probably tell you that he had kept the Mosaic Law since a child and had done all required of him, in all things. What he failed to understand is that he had done *none* of it from his *heart*, but merely from the *head*.

He did not appreciate the weight of his sin, and therefore could not appreciate how others felt about theirs. Simon's only concern was the Law - obeying and upholding it. This is what he took pride in.

Please also note that Jesus ended the conversation to the woman, with words that extended forgiveness to the woman. Certainly, this was a shocker to Simon and on another occasion, when Jesus does this same thing with another individual, the Pharisees are right there to question Him as to the validity of His claim; that He has the authority to forgive sin.

We are not speaking here of merely no longer holding something against someone else. The Pharisees would have had no problem with that. They understood that what Jesus was doing was something far greater. While it is one thing for another individual to forgive someone of an offense, that forgiveness does not move into the *legal* realm. It is nothing more than someone saying (and consequently acting as though), that they will not harbor resentment against another individual for the wrong that was committed. This action allows the relationship to continue and even grow from that point.

The problem though is that people do not have the ability to literally forgive sin, as only God can forgive. When God forgives, He sets that transgression aside, remembering it no more. He no longer holds it against us in judgment.

Our sins are only forgiven by faith in Christ and His redemptive work on Calvary's cross. Once our sins are forgiven, they are absolutely *gone*. It is as if we had never sinned. Only God can forgive sin. So, if Jesus was extending forgiveness to this woman, He was saying something about His character. He was saying that He was in fact, very God. He was telling all around Him that He was able to judicially forgive sins, because ultimately all sin is sin against God. Jesus gave the woman forgiveness because of her faith in Him, which was shown in that act of loving servitude.

The woman understood the weight of her sin and the damage it caused. She humbled herself, bought a very expensive bottle of perfume, and with tears of sorrow caused by the fact that she saw her sin for what it was, submitted herself to God in Jesus. She saw Jesus as God, very God and it was to Him she bowed in worship. The Holy Spirit had opened her eyes to the truth of His character, and she responded in brokenness, love and adoration. Her worship of Him, was fully accepted and for that, she had received salvation, which is another way of saying that her sins were forgiven her.

That this was not well received by the Pharisees and teachers of the Law goes without saying. It provided Simon with more ammunition against Jesus as the Pharisees and religious leaders built their case against Him.

Jesus spoke with authority and it was because of that authority that people had no direct retort. Jesus felt no need to prove His deity, or prove by what authority He did *anything*, in spite of the fact that the Pharisees and other religious leaders attempted to make Him feel as if He answered to them.

Chapter 12

His Work Continues

During the days following the event spoken of in our last chapter, Jesus went through the Land and continued preaching, healing, feeding the hungry, and being an example of what a life looks like when it is committed to God and His purposes. This is what Jesus came to do. He came to show humanity *why* we were created by providing a living example of a selfless, sacrificial life, and He came to live a sinless life, in order to offer Himself as a perfect propitiation for our sin. He did all of this for two reasons and two reasons only:

1. So that God's righteous anger toward sin would be appeased
2. So that God would be able to receive us to Himself

Over the entire situation, God's love was forever at work. Without His vast love for us, He never would have done what He did. Because of His holiness and justice, sin needed to be paid and it was God's perfect, infinite love that put His plan into motion; a plan which ultimately, would release all who came to Him in faith, from the bondage of sin, to life eternal.

Jesus walked this earth as a living, breathing, perfect example of God, because He was (and remains) God in the flesh. His justice, His holiness, His love, all stemmed from His natural character, which He lived as a complete human being for roughly 33 years. Everywhere He went, the essence of God was with Him, because He Himself was and is God. Everything He did, He did because He was every bit a human being, a Man, fully devoted and submitted to God's purposes being lived in and through Him.

Jesus was our example of how to *be* right with God. The problem though is that naturally born human beings are *not* right with God and it is due to the fact that we possess a sin nature; a nature that is naturally at odds with God's perfect righteousness, and His holiness. The only way to become right with God is by living a *sinless* life, which we are unable to do, because of our sin nature. Do not let people tell you that you can *arrive* to a point in this life where sin is no longer a problem. As long as we are human beings in this life, we will continue to have a sin nature. Even Christians, though made fully righteous before God, still possess that sin nature and it is that, which works against our willingness to live rightly before God that causes us to fall from time to time.

There are unfortunately, folks who firmly believe they have arrived at a state of sinless perfection. These believe that as long as they "abide" in Christ, they will remain sinless, but once they cease abiding in Christ, they sin, and are in danger of losing their salvation. When they *do* sin, they believe they lose their salvation. Due to this, they also believe they must not only repent, but also receive Christ's salvation all over again. This is a pitiful misunderstanding of the truth of God's Word.

As Paul carefully explains throughout the book of Romans, we are made righteous by our faith in Christ's shed blood, which ultimately provides us with complete victory over sin, in the next life. Paul goes through the book of Romans point by point, explaining why no one is righteous on their own, and why it takes God Himself to declare us righteous, not because of anything we have done, but because of what Christ has accomplished on our behalf. Take the time to read Romans chapters one through eight, for a solid understanding of what God in Christ has done, and how through faith, His work is appropriated to us.

The apostle John also speaks of the fact of this *abiding* in 2 John 1:9 (NET): *"Everyone who goes on ahead and does not remain in the teaching of Christ does not have God. The one who remains in this teaching has both the Father and the Son."* Please note that John is saying that those who go beyond what Christ taught, does not have Him. In other words, they *never* had Him. Abiding is taken by some to mean, *not sinning*. However, this is not the essence of the meaning of that word. The real sense of the meaning here is that the authentic Christian *remains* in Christ *because* He is in them through the Holy Spirit. The Holy Spirit's indwelling of the believer, is the believer's guarantee that they will *be able* to remain in Christ forever (cf. John 14:16ff; see also John 1:2; 1 John 4:16; 2 John 9). The oneness then, is on God. Those who are truly Christians *will* sin, but they will not sin to the point of ceasing to be Christian. God will see to that. Christ has promised never to leave or forsake us and this promise is something that He carries out.

This entire subject speaks of eternal security for each authentic Christian. This has been debated for centuries, and today as then, Christians fall on both sides of the issue, some believing that people *can* lose their salvation, while others believing that Christians cannot lost their salvation. Like many issues, no amount of debate has resolved this issue for everyone. People study, they pray, and they wind up believing one way or the other about this issue based on their understanding of Scripture.

This is a good topic to use as an example of how people think, and the results of their conclusions. One individual wrote to share his thoughts about unconditional eternal security, and stated that it, "*affords its adherents the premise (foundation) for committing all manner of sin under the blanket of a type of hell insurance policy.*"[3] The problem is that because *some* people may misinterpret the parameters of a specific biblical doctrine, and possibly abuse it due to their lack of understanding, this in no way *negates* said doctrine. They believe (wrongly, in my opinion), that because people understand this doctrine to say that the believer is safe under all circumstances, and is free to live their life as they please, sinning as much as they want to sin, this somehow proves that the doctrine itself is wrong. Not true. It would be better to say that a person who sees the doctrine in such a way, and lives his life according to his own selfish interests, has not only wrongly understood that doctrine, but there is a very real possibility that he never received authentic salvation at all.

A person, who says he believes that Jesus died for our sin, shed His blood in order to pay the penalty for that sin, rose from the dead to make salvation sure, yet chooses to live life by his own design, has *not* come to the cross. Not long ago, I had made an acquaintance via a religious forum. Normally, I tend to avoid forums because of so many

---

[3] Email from C. H. Fisher, dated 07/13/2009; 9:32 A.M.; on file

differing opinions and the trolls who often go to these boards for the sole purpose of inflicting and inciting. However, we had a few things in common and he began to email directly. I was happy to talk with him and chat about things.

He said he was a Christian, but was suffering from depression and he was having a hard time with relationships with women. A Christian suffering from depression is not beyond the norm, since clinical depression often requires medical attention since the root cause of clinical depression is often how the synapses work and how endorphins are released. A clinically depressed person's brain does not produce endorphins the way a person who does not suffer from depression does. Often, any endorphins produced in the depressed person's brain, are used up almost immediately. The result of this near-immediate depletion is fatigue, strong feelings of depression, and more. Because these endorphins are gone, there is nothing in the brain to provide the person with a sense of well being.

At any rate, we chatted back and forth for a bit and he shared more and more about himself. He mentioned his failed relationships with women. Often, these relationships involved sexual aspects. He saw nothing wrong with that and I tried to explain to him that being physical with someone he was not married to was not what God wanted. It did not honor God, nor did it help him in his relationship with Christ.

Over time, he came to disagree with me about this area and a number of other areas. In fact, it was interesting to see a number of Proverbs come true, right before my eyes. As the messenger of God's Word, I became his whipping boy. He became sarcastic, accusing me of judging him, and playing God. I was not doing this, but was instead trying to help him understand his responsibilities as a Christian. His own guilt about his lifestyle caused him to feel the way he felt. Unfortunately, I was nearby, so it was easy to take it out on me. Proverbs 9:7 (NASB), was certainly true in this situation, *"He who corrects a scoffer gets dishonor for himself, And he who reproves a wicked man gets insults for himself."*

I tried to explain things to him, because I wanted to see him grow in his faith. He would have none of it. He saw nothing wrong with his behavior and knew that God would "understand." His error in judgment and lifestyle did not cancel out the truth of the doctrine of unconditional eternal security. The plain fact of the matter is that simply because someone *claims* to be a Christian, does not in any way, shape or form, mean that he actually is a Christian. The proof is in the pudding.

Going back and forth with someone who is already set in his mind about something serves no purpose. God's truth in one form or another is always available to people. *Creation* is the testimony of God's handiwork. *Conscience* is the truth that helps us understand when we do something wrong. The *Gospel* is the truth about salvation. People either reject or receive that truth, but as long as they are alive, God has not given up on them. Either God is the One who opens someone's eyes to being receptive to the actual truth, or He does not. While we can *know* the truth, in our *heads*, God opens the hearts, allowing that truth to impact our lives. This is why we are still culpable, and still responsible for our actions. Our job is to instruct and teach, but not debate.

Chapter 13

The Thief

Certainly, one of the situations that proves the fact that God is the One who is solely responsible for bringing people to Himself is seen in the thief on the cross. Luke relays some of the time Jesus spent dying an excruciatingly painful death on the cross. On each side of Him, were two thieves. In all likelihood, they were more than just simple thieves. They were probably individuals who had been caught attempting to overthrow the Roman Empire. Their acts of thievery more than likely had something to do with treason, and the penalty for that was death. In any case, here they were, dying alongside the Author of Life. This entire scene is recorded for us in the twenty-third chapter of Luke, as well as in Matthew.

At first, both criminals are ridiculing, reviling, and accusing Christ (cf. Matthew 27:44). However, note that one of the thieves apparently reconsiders. In Luke 23:39-43, we read of the fact that one of the thieves winds up not only rebuking the other thief, but also coming to a state of repentance. In its simplest form, biblical repentance is a change of mind regarding Christ. One moment he saw Jesus as no different than he was, but one moment later, He then turns to Jesus and asks to be remembered by Him, when He comes into His kingdom.

Something or Someone opened the eyes of his heart, to the fact that Jesus was not worthy of death. However, there was more. Like Peter, who had announced that Jesus was the Christ, the Son of the living God (cf. Matthew 16:16), to which Jesus responded that his eyes had been opened by the Holy Spirit, this thief also had his eyes open the same way.

If not the Holy Spirit, then what could have opened the man's eyes? There are only two reasons that would have led up to the point when the man's eyes would have been opened to this truth:

1. He had heard Jesus asking for forgiveness for those who crucified Him, or
2. The Spirit merely opened the man's eyes because that was the Spirit's choice to do so

In either case, the Holy Spirit used either the request for forgiveness by Christ or His overall demeanor as He faced death, or the Holy Spirit used nothing, but simply chose to open the man's eyes. Whatever the case may have been, we can be sure that absolutely *no debate* took place, whereby the man was convinced to believe Jesus was the Christ, unless that debate happened only in the man's mind. We simply do not know.

The thief became a Christian, not because human arguments convinced him, but because he saw the truth, and the truth he saw went from his *head to his heart*. He believed the truth, and that truth opened the eyes of his heart, literally freeing him from the dark prison he had been in all of his life. That truth led Him to see the only One who could grant him eternal life. He saw the truth and was simply *convinced*. He *believed*. He needed no other argument. This is as close as one can get to a deathbed conversion. In truth, it is better late, than never.

Once the thief saw the truth, he did not stop it from following its natural course, which was to *affect* his decision-making faculties. Because he allowed this truth to *penetrate* his heart and his will, he simply followed that truth to its logical conclusion. That path took him right to Jesus, who he had now come to realize was *the* King over all. Unlike the Pharisees and others, the thief put up no barricade. He did not keep the truth from piercing to his inner most being. In every possible way, he *received* the truth, revealed to him by the Holy Spirit.

This is why all people are responsible for their own actions based on the amount of "light" that has been revealed to them during their life. Consistently rejecting the light that is given causes a person's conscience to harden. This hardening allows less and less truth to penetrate. Over time, as less and less truth penetrates, lies take up residence.

We waste a good deal of time using energy and effort attempting to convince people of things that only God can do. There is nothing in Scripture that tells us that part of our job is to *debate* and *work* to convince or persuade until another person "gets it." In fact, just the opposite is true.

JONAH DECIDES TO DO IT GOD'S WAY

OKAY LORD, I'LL GO!!!

©2009 F. DERUVO

As previously mentioned, Ezekiel's ministry is a perfect example of this truth because time and time again, God says to him that he must tell the house of Israel the words that God will give him...*whether they listen or not* (cf. Ezekiel 2:5, 7; 3:11, etc.). It was clearly not in Ezekiel's job description to convince anyone of the truth he was commissioned to say to Israel. It was his job to *state the truth* and that is where it ended.

Consider Jonah, as one other example. He was told by God to go to Nineveh to preach the fact that God's patience had ended and after 40 days, Nineveh would be overthrown. Jonah did not want to do that at all, so he ran. He got on a boat, headed out to sea, brought problems onto the ship and sailors, and admitted that he was the cause of the problems. By his request, they threw him overboard and God sent a huge fish to swallow Jonah, where he sat for three days and three nights to think about things. By the way, as an aside, Jesus Himself obviously believed this tale, as we see in Matthew 16:4. Enough said.

When the fish finally ejected Jonah onto dry land, Jonah did as God had originally commanded. He went to Nineveh, warned them, and guess what? They repented; *"The people of Nineveh believed in God, and they declared a fast and put on sackcloth, from the greatest to the least of them.11 3:6 When the news reached the king of Nineveh, he got up from his throne, took off his royal robe, put on sackcloth, and sat on ashes,"* (Jonah 3:5-6 NET). God saw their repentance and decided against destroying the city. Because of this, Jonah was just *not* happy! In fact, Jonah said to God, *"Oh, Lord, this is just what I thought would happen when I was in my own country. This is what I tried to prevent by attempting to escape to Tarshish! – because I knew that you are gracious and compassionate, slow to anger and abounding in mercy, and one who relents concerning threatened judgment,"* (Jonah 4:2). Apparently, Jonah did not want these people saved and told God about it. The truth of the matter though is exactly what Jonah said; that God *is* gracious, full of compassion, and willing to relent when people turn to him in true repentance.

Here is a case of God using a prophet who did not *want* to be a prophet. Can you imagine how half-heartedly he might have preached, although he could have also preached out of his anger at them? He certainly did not want them saved. Despite what Jonah wanted, God wanted something else entirely, and He brought it about, in spite of Jonah.

Our job as authentic Christians is to preach the Word, to tell people about salvation. Our job is to put the truth out there and God will use it to bring glory to Himself. Our responsibility goes no further than ensuring that we tell people the truth, the whole truth and nothing but the truth, where the Gospel is concerned. By the way, our "telling" them does not merely involve words. It involves *actions*, and *attitudes*, and ultimately, our *life*.

Anyone can preach. Anyone can use words to sound good, but it takes someone who has the authentic character of Christ within them, that enables them to *live* a life that speaks of their own salvation. It does not matter what we actually say or do, if the truth of Christ is not in us. That truth should be living, growing, and bringing us to maturity.

We can all point to individuals who have spent their adult lives preaching something, but then some undercover journalist goes behind the veil they have created, and we see them for who they are, and it is usually not a pleasant sight. We feel violated, especially if we were gullible enough to believe their words. Now, we see their true character, as purveyors of error, born out of selfish ambition to become rich. Too many people blame God or Christianity for this, when in point of fact, this should be chalked up to the fact that Christ told us way ahead of time that *tares* would be sewn with the wheat (cf. Matthew 13). These fakers are just that; individuals *pretending* to be authentic Christians, when in reality, they are nothing but predators. Because their own consciences are seared, they have no ability to recognize their own error. They are wolves and they must be avoided, because they will give no heed to truth.

One thief on the cross came face to face with the truth and reacted accordingly. He saw himself as unworthy, filled with grief over his own sinfulness. He looked to Another, the only One who could extricate him from the pit. The truth he saw was found in Christ and that truth was the only truth that could effectively save him.

It was not debating the truth *into* the thief that caused a change of heart. God revealed His truth about Christ to the man, which prompted him to realize his need for Christ. The thief, instead of rejecting that truth out of hand, *embraced* it. He embraced it, because he was willing to be humbled by it. Because he was humbled by it, repentance came from it, leading him all the way to Jesus.

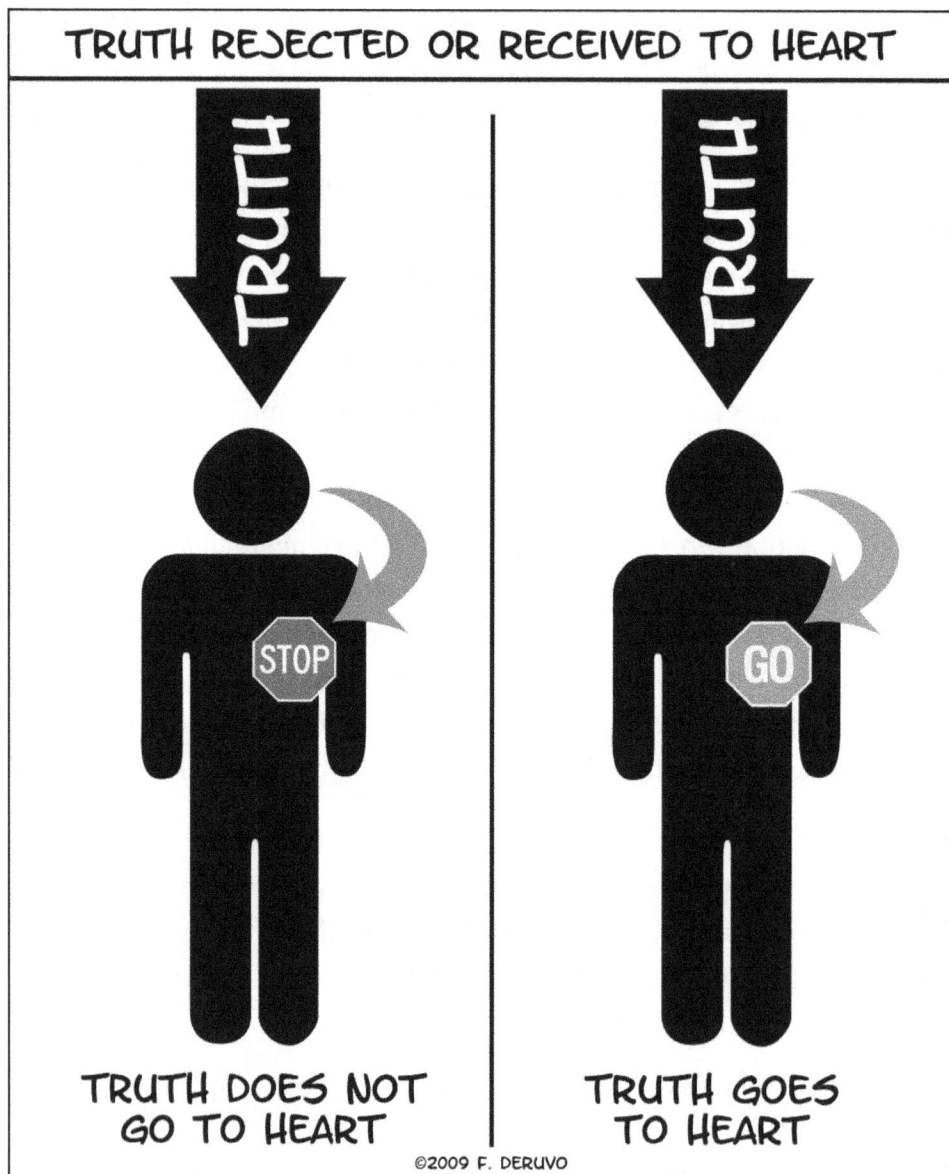

TRUTH REJECTED OR RECEIVED TO HEART

TRUTH

TRUTH

STOP

GO

TRUTH DOES NOT
GO TO HEART

TRUTH GOES
TO HEART

©2009 F. DERUVO

Chapter 14

It's Lame...

One of the first books I published is called *The Anti-Supernatural Bias of Ex-Christians*. People seem to enjoy it, unless they are atheists or ex-Christians (which is a misnomer). These folks are convinced that God does not at all exist.

In that book, part of it was spent analyzing another book written by a man who firmly believes that he *was* – at one time – a *committed Christian*. In fact, he was a preacher, until he arrived at a certain understanding, which was the impetus for his resolve to stop being a

Christian. It took place over a number of years, and he relates the events that led up to his ultimate rejection of Jesus and Christianity. He now contends that he is a well-adjusted atheist. That sounds like an oxy-moron. However, it gets even more interesting.

What is interesting is that he *"knows"* beyond doubt that he *was* at one point, a Christian. At the same time, he *now* knows, just as strongly, that he is in fact, *now* an atheist. You read that correctly. He *knows* God does not now exist (and never existed), but when he refers to the time he was a Christian, he knew beyond doubt that God did exist. Never let it be said that atheists make sense, because they do not. In spite of this, they persist in their illogical ways, yet have the temerity to refer to the Christian and Christianity with unchecked arrogance.

When *The Anti-Supernatural Bias of Ex-Christians* was published, I sent the author of the book I had reviewed, a copy of it. He was not at all impressed with it, and in effect, called it "lame." That was fine. While there was hope that he might see truth in my words, there was no guarantee that he would. In fact, there was little hope that he would see truth, as he seemed pretty set in his atheistic ways. God provides truth, but man can and does reject it.

Within just a few days of publication through Amazon, the book started selling. Within two or three weeks after that, a few individuals had placed up reviews. The reviews were interesting. The first one said this:

> *"This is one of the poorest argued books of this type I have read. If you want to read a book that completely undermines what is expressed in this 'book', see Dan Barker's "Godless". Barker was an evangelical preacher who desired to really find out the facts as they are, not as he wanted them to be - and came to lose his once firmly held faith."*

Another one, posted within a few days of the first one said this:

> *"In his foreword, DeRuvo states that: 'I hope ultimately though, that you will realize the futility and foolishness of those who say that God does not exist, and that you will come to see the truth.' His book is an attempt to bring ex-Christians (atheists) back to Christianity. His arguments are circular, frequently relying on a "this is what the Bible says" approach. DeRovo's (sic) book is illogical and philosophically childish."*

The review was annoying, but not because someone disliked the book. I did not care about that at all. It was annoying because it seemed like a case of two atheists simply wanting to preach their negativity regarding the contents of the book because it had to do with Christianity. This seems often to be the case on Amazon, where atheists "review" Christian-related books by castigating either the book or the author, or both. They likely hope that others who might be considering the book, will consider no more. The atheist reviewers will try to push the public to some other book, more to their liking.

It seems very apparent that neither one of these individuals actually read *The Anti-Supernatural Bias of Ex-Christians*. The number one reason the book was written was to address concerns I had regarding the whole phenomenon of the "Christian-turned-atheist." Reviewing the book by the minister-turned-atheist was simply part of the process. His words, actions and the events in his life were compared with God's Word. There was *no* attempt to prove God exists, nor was there an attempt to prove Christianity is viable or valid. All I did was look at the atheist's book, find out what his view of Scripture was, and see if his arguments held up under the microscope of Scripture. Since he claimed to have been a Christian, then to compare his life and beliefs with the Bible is nothing out of the ordinary.

For instance, the atheist-author admitted in his book that he is a skeptic by nature. I would say he is actually a cynic, but we will leave it at that. Because of his skepticism, he tends to approach the subject of the supernatural much the way James Randi (the Amazing Randi) does when he comes across people who claim to be psychics. Randi normally attempts to replicate *exactly* what the psychics do, but Randi does it by *avoiding* the supernatural altogether. In essence, he sets out to prove that every psychic ability or phenomenon has a *natural* explanation, as opposed to a supernatural one. Watching Randi work is fascinating actually, and he has uncovered many alleged psychics, who turned out to be nothing more than complete fakes.

Therefore, the atheist-author insists that like Randi, he also is skeptical of anything that is supernatural. The atheist-author then sets out to prove that the Bible is devoid of the supernatural. How does he do this? Unlike Randi, who would attempt to replicate the events of Scripture *without* changing them, this particular atheist-author set about to disprove any supernatural connection with Scripture by essentially *re-writing* some of the events of the Bible that he did not feel were believable.

Instead of recreating the events that purportedly happened in the Bible, he merely rewrites the narratives, so that he is satisfied that the way he has written it is the way it actually happened. That is swell, however, that is *not* what the Amazing Randi would have done.

One of the examples that the atheist-author attempts to "clarify" is the experience of the apostle Paul on the island of Malta (cf. Acts 27-28). Here, for those who are familiar with the incident, we know that Paul and the others shipwrecked on the island due to a storm, which caused the boat to crash against the rocks. While there, they started a fire to dry their clothing and keep warm.

During the process of gathering wood and starting the fire, we read that a viper, which has apparently wakened due to the heat of the fire, reached out, bit Paul and hung on to him. Paul simply shook the viper off his hand and into the fire. Some of the natives of the island saw what happened and waited for Paul to die from the effects of the bite. When he did not, these same natives began to assume that Paul was some kind of god.

The atheist-author rewrote this event into something more to his liking. He admitted he did not believe it happened like that, so he took the liberty of adjusting the narrative to suit him. He said he searched and found that "most" snakes when they bite, coil, attack, bite, then recoil, ready for another strike if necessary. He was not at all sure about a snake hanging onto Paul's hand. That was so very *not* believable.

In my book, I researched and found out that there are a number of vipers, which actually *do* bite and hang on. They hang on so that more of their venom is released into their victim's body. It is not as out of the ordinary, as our atheist-author friend would like us to believe.

The atheist-author rewrote the Bible to suit himself because he says he is a skeptic. My point is that he did not need to rewrite anything, and he could *still* eliminate the supernatural. Let us say that this type of snake had bitten Paul many times over the course of his life. If so, then naturally Paul would have built up immunity to the snake's venom. Without changing one thing about the narrative, I provided a natural reason for why Paul might not have died. Now, for this to be fact, it would have to proven that Paul encountered this type of viper many times, either by going to Malta, or by encountering this type of viper in other areas of the world. We do not know if this is the case and it was probably *not* the case.

The analysis of the atheist's book showed the absence of quality research, resulting in illogical claims by the author. The two individuals who "reviewed" my book assumed that they knew what I was saying in my book and did not even need to read it, apparently. The trouble is that their comments are so general, that their reviews could apply to *any* book that argues against the atheist position. Since mine was not written against the atheist position, but was written to expose their lack of understanding of the biblical narrative, their "reviews" of my book simply do not fit.

I understand at the start that atheists will not like my book, but whether they think so or not, it was not written *to them* or *for them*. It was written for Christians who are interested in finding out about this growing phenomenon called "ex-Christians." I show from Scripture that this should not be something that takes Christians by surprise. Christ warned us of it in the Parable of the Wheat and the Tares as well as elsewhere. Both Paul and Peter tell us that in the last days, there will be a falling away (cf. 1 & 2 Thessalonians), and that in the last days, people will be proud, boastful, arrogant, etc. (cf. 2 Peter 3). This truth exists, so when we hear of people "falling away" from the faith, it should sadden us, but *not* surprise us.

No amount of debating or arguing will convince these people that they are a living tragedy, and fulfillment of Scripture. They are convinced otherwise; that they *now* have the truth and that God does not exist. Moreover, Christians are considered to be deluded by these same individuals, who will tell you that at one time in their lives, they prayed, read the Bible, preached, maybe spoke in tongues, did what they could to help people and all the rest. To them, it does not matter if they were not an authentic Christian from the start. They will become incensed if someone deigns to tell them that they were not actual Christians in the first place.

The truth is that an authentic Christian is one not because he believes the story of Jesus (as some of these ex-Christians state), but because there was a new birth, which gave him salvation, and created within him a newness that only comes from that new birth; the birth from above.

Salvation does *not* mean believing a story of Jesus. Anyone can believe a story about a person. What does that really mean? Salvation stems from believing *in* Jesus' *efficacy*. It is what He and He alone has accomplished for the sinner in need of repentance, leading to salvation. Authentic Christians place their faith *in* Christ, His Words, His promises, His deeds, His atonement. It is that faith in those things that allows a new creation to occur within each individual Christian.

Chapter 15

Those Fabulous Religious Leaders

Jesus never seemed to enjoy a moment's peace from the Pharisees and other religious leaders. They constantly hounded, questioned, accused, and berated Jesus. In most cases, Jesus merely continued, minding His Father's business. It was normally the Pharisees, or Sadducees who tracked Him down, watched Him work, and then sought to accuse Him about something.

In the eleventh chapter of Luke, we read of another one of those situations in which Jesus did was He was put here to accomplish, and suffered the wrath of the opposition because of it. It is an interesting verbal interchange to be sure.

> *"Now he was casting out a demon that was mute. When the demon had gone out, the man who had been mute began to speak, and the crowds were amazed. But some of them said, "By the power of Beelzebul, the ruler of demons, he casts out demons." Others, to test him, began asking for a sign from heaven. But Jesus, realizing their thoughts, said to them, "Every kingdom divided against itself is destroyed, and a divided household falls. So if Satan too is divided against himself, how will his kingdom stand? I ask you this because you claim that I cast out demons by Beelzebul. Now if I cast out demons by Beelzebul, by whom do your sons cast them out?* (Luke 11:14-19, NET)

Here is Jesus, taking care of His Father's business, freeing a son of Israel from the power of the evil one, and is accused of using Satan's power to cast out a follower of Satan! Not only is this illogical, but *blasphemous*, if in fact, it was by God's power that Christ cast out the demon! Whoever was objecting (the text merely says, *"some of them said,"* though it is probably a small group of religious leaders; Scribes, Pharisees, or Sadducees), did not like the fact that Jesus was doing something that they were *not* doing. At every turn, this Jesus was grabbing all the attention for Himself! How frustrating that must have been for the haughty religious leaders.

The text states that Jesus "realized" their thoughts. From that, we can determine that either Jesus had exceptional hearing, or He understood *supernaturally* what they were mumbling about to themselves. In either case, they did not have the gumption to accuse Him directly to His face, regarding these concerns they harbored. They likely wanted other people around them to hear their comments, and pick up the chant, joining in their disbelief.

Without skipping a beat, Jesus cuts to the chase and points right back at them. He candidly reveals two things:

1. *Their lack of knowledge*
2. *Their hypocrisy*

These individuals lacked the basic understanding of logic. If Satan (Beelzebul) was actually directing his own minions to possess people, then giving a human being the power to cast the demon(s) out of those same people, his house would have been divided. It made no sense, and it would soon crumble. This was true anyway, as Satan was as good as defeated, but Jesus was pointing it out for those who were hard of hearing or dull-witted when it came to understanding Scripture.

Christ then pointed the flood light directly on the hypocrisy of His accusers. On one hand, they were willing to accuse Jesus of using satanic power to cast out demons. On the other hand, some of their followers also cast out demons. Whose power did *they* use? If the accusers said that it was God's power, then of course, Jesus would follow that up with "How do you know, and how is it your followers are not casting out with Satan's power?" They would be caught in their own web, so Jesus' accusers remained quiet.

As Jesus continued to work among the people, more incidents came to the fore, pitting Christ against these religious leaders. It got to the point where it became too obvious not to acknowledge that Jesus was doing things that others could not replicate. That did not matter to Jesus. He was doing the Father's will and nothing would keep Him from that.

The religious leaders, the doubters, those who scorned Christ and others, all wanted more from Him. They wanted a sign. In Luke 11:29ff, Jesus has already done many, many things in view of these unbelievers, but it was apparently not enough. They had the mendacity to demand a sign. Christ told them that they would be given no sign, except the sign of Jonah. According to Scripture, we know that Jonah was in the belly of the large fish for three days and three nights. Jesus was saying that this was the only sign they were getting. What is absurd about this entire conversation is that *everything* Jesus did was virtually a sign, testifying to His deity and Messiahship! Yet, here they wanted a "sign on demand." *"Unless we get a sign on demand, we will not believe,"* is what they were saying. The truth is that they would have found some reason for not believing anyway, even if He *had* provided them with a sign at their insistence. This was merely another attempt by the enemy to push Jesus *beyond* the Father's will, prompting Him to use His deity for something *other* than the Father's perfect will.

Instead of reminding them of all the things He had already done, Jesus simply pointed them to the *future*, to the time when He would die, spend three days and three nights in the grave, and then rise again. Just as Jonah was "resurrected" from the fish, by being vomited onto dry land, so Jesus would rise from the dead, because neither the grave nor death would be able to keep Him there.

Just a few verses later, in the same chapter of Luke, we read of another incident in which Jesus received an invitation to dinner by yet another Pharisee. According to the text, the Pharisee was flabbergasted to see that Jesus did not wash His hands prior to eating. Jesus used this as an opportune time to teach another lesson about the cleanliness of the soul.

The Pharisees were concerned with exteriors, but Jesus rightly pointed out that these Pharisees were religious fanatics, solely worrying about the way things *looked*. The problem was that they were concerned about how things looked on the outside, but had no concern how things on the inside looked...to *God*.

Jesus was careful not to ignore the fact that the Pharisees, the religious leaders and teachers of the Law, concerned themselves with being properly attired, properly saluted in the marketplace, and properly following all the external ceremonial aspects of the Law. They loved it when people literally bowed to them in public places. They thrilled to the idea that the common person looked up to them. They enjoyed their station in life, in spite of the fact that they were the blind leading the blind.

Jesus powerfully rebuked them, and they deserved it, because apart from a few like Nicodemus, the religious leaders opposed Jesus at every turn, regardless of the fact that Jesus had the truth they so desperately needed, and was the Messiah they were seeking. No amount of truth expressed by Jesus would, or could convince them of the error of their ways. They were not open to it. They simply refused to hear and consider the possibility that Jesus was the "One" for which Israel had been waiting. Their complete lack of faith kept their eyes from seeing that truth. They remained forever in the shadows while Christ walked this earth. For all intents and practices, they remained in outer darkness, which is where they await their divine appointment with God for judgment. That is terrifying beyond measure to consider, and to think, the Truth walked and lived among them. The Truth came, offering the Way and the Life, but He was rejected at every turn from those who should have known better, but could not see beyond the letter of the Law to behold the absolute fulfillment of the Law.

At least one of these religious leaders tried a different tack with Christ, by telling Him that He was hurting their feelings when He said these terrible things about them (cf. Luke 11:45). However, instead of backing down, Jesus went full bore and really opened up on them, accusing them not only of making it exceedingly difficult (if not impossible) for anyone to enter into the true way, and not wanting to enter in themselves! They were content to have the adoration and respect of the people, instead of doing what their position required of them; leading people out of darkness, to the light, by teaching them the truth. They could not teach the truth, since they could not *see* the truth! Immediately after this event, those opposed to Christ (religious leaders, Pharisees, etc.), decided to find a way to trap Him. They needed to stop him, and finding a way to kill Him seemed the only logical solution.

Not once during any of these encounters has Jesus entered into debate with these men. He responded to their attempted rebukes with truth. He ostracized Himself from them by living and teaching nothing but the truth. Truth backed them into a corner, and as animals that fear capture, they fought back with all they had. Their goal was to get rid of this Christ, to remove Him from the scene. Surely, there must be a way to entrap Him, ending His public ministry. This then endeavored to do.

Merely a few chapters later in Luke, Jesus did something that again brought an outcry against Him from those within the religious arena. This time it was at a synagogue when Jesus expressed compassion on a woman who was bent over with an infirmity. She was unable to straighten herself up, so Jesus healed her (cf. Luke 13:10-17). Well, my goodness, you would have thought that Jesus had done something terrible, because Luke tells us, "*...the president of the synagogue, indignant because Jesus had healed on the Sabbath, said to the crowd, 'There are six days on which work should be done! So come and be healed on those days, and not on the Sabbath day',*" (Luke 13:14).

Instead of seeing the good in what Jesus had just done, this person was intent upon complaining about it. So blind was he that he was unable to know and appreciate a true miracle when he saw it himself! *"No one is going to be healed in MY synagogue on the Sabbath!! Got it?!"* This was the letter of the Law at work in this man's heart, not the compassion of God. However, to show just how absurd this man's outburst had been, we read in verses 15 and 16, Jesus rebukes him with *"You hypocrites!*

Does not each of you on the Sabbath untie his ox or his donkey from its stall, and lead it to water? Then shouldn't this woman, a daughter of Abraham whom Satan bound for eighteen long years, be released from this imprisonment on the Sabbath day?"

Of course what Jesus is saying is that not one person present would have a problem if they saw another Jewish person lead one of their own animals to water, or pull it out if it a pit from which it had fallen, even if this had been on a Sabbath. They would *not* wait until the Sabbath was over, in order to do what was *good* and *right* to their animals. Yet, this woman, who was infinitely more valuable than any animal was essentially being told that she should have waited for healing until *after* the Sabbath! The reaction to His words tells us all we need to know: *"When he said this all his adversaries were humiliated, but the entire crowd was rejoicing at all the wonderful things he was doing,"* (Luke 13:17). Jesus' words had no positive effect on the religious leaders at all. Not only did it *not* help them see the truth of their fallen condition, but His words also caused them to become even more emphatic about the need to eradicate this Jesus. Israel was not big enough for the religious leaders *and* Jesus.

The Pharisees had tried many things to silence Jesus, but in Luke 13:31b, they tell Jesus to *"Get away from here, because Herod wants to kill you."* Huh? Wait a minute. These people who opposed Jesus at every turn, now all of a sudden seem to be concerned about His welfare? It is more likely that they were simply trying to make Jesus think that His life was in danger, so that He would run. Christ knew better.

Chapter 16

Questioning Jesus' Authority

SEE HERE...BY WHAT AUTHORITY DO YOU BELIEVE YOU CAN COME IN HERE AND DEMAND TO SEE MY FINANCIAL STATEMENTS?

©2009 F. DERUVO

Toward the end of Jesus' life, the Pharisees became desperate. They questioned everything, and kept silent when Jesus questioned them. They demanded answers from Him, but gave none in return.

In Luke 20:1-8, there is a very candid exchange between these so-called religious leaders, and Jesus. One day, Jesus was busy teaching the people in the Temple courts. While He taught, the religious leaders came up to Him, and posed a simple question. As seen in verse two, the question was *"Tell us: By what authority are you doing these things? Or who it is who gave you this authority?"* A simple question to be sure, however, Christ knew that looks could be deceiving and that was certainly the case in this instance. Jesus knew that if He said His authority came from the Father, they would accuse Him of blasphemy, not even considering the possibility that Jesus' authority *did* come from the Father! To the religious leaders, this was beyond the realm of possibility.

Instead of playing into their hands, Jesus asked a question of them. The question was also a simple one; *"John's baptism – was it from heaven or from people?"* Is that a remarkable question, or what? The import of the question did not go unnoticed by the religious leaders either. Immediately, they began discussing their options:

> *"If we say, 'From heaven,' he will say, 'Why did you not believe him?' But if we say, 'From people,' all the people will stone us, because they are convinced that John was a prophet.' So they replied that they did not know where it came from."* (Luke 20:5-7)

You see, these men were not stupid. They were simply blind. They worked their way through the problem and realized that if they said John's baptism came from above, then Jesus would demand them to answer why they did not believe John, and if they said his baptism came from people, then the people could become upset at them, which could lead to their death, literally. When Jesus asked about John's baptism, He was asking about the authority that John had to do and say the things he did and said. Where did his authority come from, in other words? The religious leaders were now asking Jesus the same question about His own authority.

You have to delight in Jesus' response to their comment here. Please note that again, Jesus does not enter into debate with these individuals.

They said simply "We do not know" where John's authority came from, but they were lying and Jesus proves to us that He knows they are lying, when He simply states, *"Neither will I tell you by whose authority I do these things,"* (Luke 20:8). Please notice that Jesus is saying two things to them:

1. You are lying and I know you are lying
2. Because you refuse to tell me and face the consequences, neither will I tell you

It is *masterful*. Jesus avoids getting into an argument with these pretenders. He did not live life only to be sidetracked by arguing over endless genealogies and words. He is here to do the work that the Father sent Him to complete.

It is exceedingly easy to allow ourselves to be caught up into situations, which serve no good purpose. It is easy because it is often a thing of pride. Part of us certainly wants others to know the truth. Another part of us wants to be *right*, and when someone says we are not right, that gets our dander up. We must prove to that other individual that we are in fact *right* and they would be wise to get that through their thick head. Hence, we muscle our way onward, breaking down doors, ready to beat people over the head with our biblical viewpoint, and if all else fails, we will call them names, or attack them in some other way. It is all to help them understand that they are blind and we can see 20/20. They must realize this, or perish, we tell ourselves.

Now when this does not work, we tend to approach the situation more pragmatically, looking soulfully through wistful eyes at the individual who fails to see us as a prophet. As such, we are here to warn them of the dire consequences of their failure to hear the truth we present. What it all boils down to is pride, plain and simple though. In the email discussion I had with an individual who rejects the eternal security of the believer, he chastised me for my "worldly viewpoint." He implored me to repent, stating, "*Fred, it is not too late to repent and seek forgiveness. Like Blackstone, you can come to the knowledge of the truth and renounce your book and other [Pretribulation Rapture] promotions. I implore you to turn off the secular music, the Internet, and spend some time in prayer and fasting. If nothing else comes of it but conviction of having sown strife and discord, you will have gained. No man can hear God who imbibes the secular spirits of the world system.*"[4]

In yet another email, he indicated that I was a heretic and in definite danger of eternal doom and damnation. So when it all comes down to it, what people do when a particular viewpoint is not accepted, is to resort to name-calling, or other ad hominem attacks.

In fact, it is not at all difficult to find forums or books where this is a regular occurrence. People do not like to be wrong, so when they firmly believe that they *are not* wrong, yet the other individual will not listen to reason, then the only way they can make themselves feel better, is by labeling the person who does not accept their opinion (seen as truth), as a heretic. Once the opposition is so labeled, then they cease to be a person, becoming someone who is completely blind. Because they are now seen as someone who is fully deluded and deceived, then the only thing left is to feign sincere sorrow for the individual. "*I know that I'm right. I just wish that God would open their eyes to the lies they believe. Oh, how it breaks my heart!*"

Do you know how many people do this? Jehovah's Witnesses, Mormons, Preterists, Dispensationalists, Covenant Theologians, and the list goes on. Everyone who is strong in their own particular set of beliefs, at some point will come to a realization that the other person, who will not budge, needs sympathy because they are deceived. Either they will go to that extreme, or they will become prideful about their own position. In either case, pride is often the root.

---

[4] Email from C. H. Fisher, dated 07/12/2009; 7:41 P.M.; on file

There is no room for pride in the life of the Christian. There is really no room for error either; however, there are some theological perspectives, which offer us a bit of "wiggle room" from one to the other. There is no wiggle room when discussing the deity of Christ, the Trinity, salvation by faith alone, and a few other areas. Paul makes this clear in his letter to the Corinthians, when some believe they should not eat certain foods, or set a specific day aside to the Lord, while to others, every day is special, etc., (cf. 1 Corinthians 8:1-15; 10:23ff).

Chapter 17
Shunning Foolish Controversies

P aul taught the early Church many things and thankfully, a good deal of what he taught has been incorporated into what is today called, the Bible. When he wrote to the Corinthians, he discussed the myriad of problems they had, from licentious living style, to other social problems with divisions. They were worldly, carnal, not evidencing the truth in Christ. Paul had to take the time to correct them on any number of things.

Whenever he wrote, he normally offered insight and correction where necessary. Two individuals whom he looked to as sons – Timothy and Titus – were especially privy to his instruction. In his letters – referred to as Pastoral Epistles – Paul informs these two young men how they should live, not simply as Christians, but as pastors of the Lord's flock.

One of the things he pointed out to them concerned controversies. Paul was very clear, because it was important for him to teach that becoming embroiled in controversies will soon enough, keep a person from being involved in the Lord's work. Satan would love nothing more than for Christians (either professing or authentic), to be constantly at each other's throats over doctrine. While of course, it is supremely important to have correct biblical viewpoints, we must also realize that we do not convince anyone of anything. Every word we speak might be absolute truth, but if people reject it, that truth does nothing for them.

> *"But avoid foolish controversies, genealogies, quarrels, and fights about the law, because they are useless and empty. Reject a divisive person after one or two warnings. You know that such a person is twisted by sin and is conscious of it himself,"* (Titus 3:9-11 NET).

Paul's words seen above explain a number of things to young Titus. The words tell Titus to avoid:

- *Foolish controversies*
- *Genealogies*
- *Quarrels*
- *Fights about the Law*

Why should Titus avoid these things? As Paul says, they are *useless* and *empty*. Paul even goes so far as to tell Titus that someone who is purposefully divisive should be avoided after one or two warnings. That person is "twisted by sin." People who want nothing more than to argue and debate have a problem. Their problem is that they do not care about people. They care only about being right. They want to expose what they believe is error in you, so that they can feel good about *themselves*. This is nothing more than pride, which does nothing except to puff up. It gives people a false sense of importance, as if they themselves are their own teacher. Paul also discusses this same type of situation with Timothy (cf. 1 Timothy 1:3-7).

People like this always seem to come down on others who read commentaries, or study what others believe. They are self-made people, who have come by their teaching directly from the Holy Spirit! How dare anyone question them as to their beliefs! How dare anyone imply that what he or she believes is wrong! The Holy Spirit *Himself* taught those people therefore they cannot be wrong! Nevertheless, the problem is that this type of person has absolutely no accountability. They are not under the authority of anyone else. They do not allow anyone to tell them, or suggest to them that their beliefs may in fact, be aberrant. This is an unacceptable conclusion and is rejected out of hand.

What is also interesting is that many of these same people have no professional education. They have merely opened the Bible and begun learning. Now certainly, there is nothing wrong with that, however, there comes a time when all of us come to the end of our ability to learn, and therefore must rely on others, who are more learned in a particular field.

For instance, I have studied Greek, but I am not an expert. Therefore, I must rely on others who are actual experts. However, if all I do is look at one Greek lexicon from one Greek-speaking teacher, I am not doing any favors to myself or anyone else. I must avail myself of as many lexicons as possible to become saturated with the possible definitions of a word. A person's credentials must also come into play when deciding on a particular meaning.

Some men whom God has raised up are experts in one field or another. However, to hear some tell it, God does not want me to avail myself of their teaching. Only the Holy Spirit should teach me. Just Him and me, and the Bible.

Nevertheless, in truth, if we only need the Holy Spirit, then one has to wonder why the Bible is needed. Could not this same Holy Spirit write a Bible just for me? Does He actually need the apostles, the prophets, and others originally used by God to pen God's Word?

For some reason, the Holy Spirit has chosen to use men to write the Bible, for all of us to use. He has raised up others who specialize in languages, or histories, or archaeology, or something else entirely. The Holy Spirit raised these people up in order to edify those within the Body of Christ. We are all to benefit one another, yet some live as though it is just them and God. They need nothing else. They do not need fellowship. They do not need to sit under the preaching of a shepherd. They do not need to pray with others. They only need the Holy Spirit. However, this is not what God designed and what they fail to see is that their position is born purely of pride, and nothing else. While they firmly believe that they are in fact, approaching life *scripturally*, and therefore, spiritually, they are doing the furthest thing from it.

God did not intend for us to be alone. This is seen in the Garden of Eden, and that was before Adam had even sinned, yet it was not good for Adam to be alone. How much more do we need fellowship now that we are fallen, *though* saved?

Paul speaks to Titus, explaining to him the pitfalls of dealing with factious people. They are a major thorn in the side and should be avoided. People in general should *not* be avoided. Factious people should be warned once or twice, and *then* avoided. They only seek their own, and they want to suck you in with them, so that they become *your* teacher and you will always be the student.

Cult leaders have this ability. They use their strength of pride/ego to ensure that people will not question them. They force their viewpoints on others and people simply accept what they have to say because of the way in which they say it. There is no room for disagreement.

Think about people that you may know who have an air of authority. When they provide an answer, it is generally accepted because of the way it is presented. It does not even matter if they are right or not. What often matters is *how* they present their response. The level of authority they use determines how well their response is accepted as truth.

Con artists rely on this type of demeanor to accomplish their goals. In a sense, if a pastor or Bible teacher tends to lord it over others, in one way or another, he does so in order to avoid being questioned by the flock. If they can make themselves appear to be above being questioned, then no one *will* question them and it is not long before people believe whatever they say. This is why cults often do not start out as cults. They often start out as a group of people who have a common belief in Christ. There is joy, love, and appreciation for one another. Everyone looks up to the leader because he is normally intelligent, knowledgeable, approachable (to an extent), and always seems to know how to handle a situation. People feel comfortable placing themselves under that individual's authority. In fact, they begin to relish it because they believe that this person has something to offer them that they could not otherwise have themselves, apart from him.

The tragedy is that over time, these followers forget how to think for themselves, and the leader becomes more and more unwilling to answer questions. He simply promotes his ideas as *law*. This law is to be carried out verbatim and if not, there will be consequences. We have seen this with people like David Koresh, Jim Jones and many others. We shake our head with wonder at how people could allow themselves to be controlled like that, but we forget that often, people do not know why they believe, so they look to someone who seems to know. Because they build this relationship with this person over time, they begin to feel incredibly guilty if they start to have doubts about them.

This is why Paul says that a factious person should be avoided at all costs. They are showing that they are *unwilling* to listen to, or be corrected by, others. They have all the knowledge there is and their job is to share it with you. They in effect, have stopped growing spiritually because they have already arrived at that point, in which they are heads above all others. They are often very articulate people, with a large vocabulary and seem to have an extreme amount of patience, never allowing their feathers to become ruffled, at least at first. These people are dangerous in many ways, because they consider themselves spiritual giants and leaders; often godlike. People like this do not accept correction, do not hesitate to tell you when you are wrong, and will do whatever it takes to maintain their own view of themselves, and position they hold, so that others will continue to trust them.

If we take the time to look at the book of Acts, we will see that time and time again, Jewish men (and sometimes, women), came together to oppose Paul and his ministry partners. They could not let go of the past, nor could they see any good in this new Christian movement; something they referred to derogatorily as the "Way." Paul would attempt on every occasion to witness to them, trying to help them see that their beliefs and ways were at odds with the revealed will of God. In spite of how much Paul (or someone else) attempted to correct their errant viewpoint, they could not see it. This often resulted in their becoming extremely angry with the messenger, and that led to stoning, or attempted killings, beatings, or something else entirely.

In Acts chapters seven and eight, we read of Stephen, who became the first martyr. In this chapter, he attempts to help these religious leaders and rulers see and understand that they believed in something that had no efficacy. He was trying to point them to the fact that the entirety of the Law found fulfillment in Jesus Christ. They would have none of it. They would not give up their lie, to believe the truth. They would not repent. The more they heard, the angrier they became.

Finally, at one point, in the middle of his speech, Stephen himself becomes angered. He turns from explanation to accusation and states, *"You stubborn people, with uncircumcised hearts and ears! You are always resisting the Holy Spirit, like your ancestors did! Which of the prophets did your ancestors not persecute? They killed those who foretold long ago the coming of the Righteous One, whose betrayers and murderers you have now become! You received the law by decrees given by angels, but you did not obey it,"* (Acts 7:51-53).

The result of this was Stephen's death by stoning. The religious leaders would not take comeuppance from some snot-nosed kid (compared to them and their age), who had no respect for their position in life! They were unable to hear the truth, because they preferred the lie that kept them in their esteemed position in life.

After Christ saved Saul on the road to Damascus, he who had been an earnest enemy of the cross had now become its most ardent supporter. This put Paul in the position of receiving more persecution than any normal man could bear up under. Certainly, Paul would say that it was only by God's grace and strength that held him up at all, and that is true. The reality is that wherever he went after his conversion, he always preached to the Jews first, and then if they rejected his message, he took it to the Gentiles.

The Jewish men who rejected Paul's message did so because they were not even *willing* to look at their own beliefs, in order to determine whether what Paul stated was true. You get the impression that even if they thought for a moment that what Paul said might have been true, they did not want to listen anyway. This then gave way to severe hatred and anger, which when left unchecked, became murderous.

Paul knew when to stop talking to people. He knew when the discussion was over and it was becoming counter-productive. Paul knew that people should be told the message and the results should be left up to Holy God. God would be the One who opened the eyes, or left them alone.

Had Paul tried to convince through debate, a good deal of time would have been wasted. Paul had a job to do and that job was to tell people about salvation that came only from Jesus Christ. No amount of convincing people to repent and believe would *cause* them to repent and believe.

Paul would present the truth and let the chips fall where they would fall. Some believed, most rejected. Some tried to be polite in their rejection, while others acted rudely and ignorantly as they rejected. One cannot help but wonder that if Paul had stopped to debate with people about this, that or the other thing, he would probably still be in Cyprus (cf. Acts 13).

Christ issued the Great Commission in Matthew 28:16-20. There, Christ says to us, *"...go and make disciples of all nations, baptizing them in the name of the Father and the Son and the Holy Spirit, teaching them to obey everything I have commanded you. And remember, I am with you always, to the end of the age."*

Our job as Christians is to *tell people.* Our job is *not* to convince. That is the job of the Holy Spirit and if we see anything in Scriptures, we see where God at times, turned people to repentance, and at other times, no repentance was evident. God opens the eyes of the blind as He will, and He has chosen to use us to spread His Word to the world. Nowhere in our job description are we responsible for *convincing* anyone that only

Christ holds the truth. Nowhere are we told that we must tell *and* persuade.

There were times in the gospels when people who began following Jesus, ultimately rejected and left Him. There were times when Christ Himself, gave people the truth, only to see them reject it. There is no guarantee that people will hear the truth and be convinced. The only guarantee we have is that somewhere, certain people will receive the truth, and it may be because we said something. It may have to do with the fact that we *did* something, or it may be due to the fact that God merely opened their heart to the truth, seeing their repentance (change in attitude and demeanor toward Him).

In preparing Ezekiel for his mission to the house of Israel, God told him a number of things in preparation. One of the things He said was, *"Those who listen will listen, but the indifferent will refuse, for they are a rebellious house,"* (Ezekiel 3:27). At the same time, God specifically told Ezekiel that if he failed to tell people about their coming fate, and they died in their iniquity, they would be held accountable for their sin, but Ezekiel's blood would also be required. If Ezekiel told people of their coming fate due to their iniquity, and they did not yield to his instruction, and died in their iniquity, they would be held accountable for their sin, but Ezekiel would be free from responsibility (cf. Ezekiel 3:16ff; etc.).

The truth of the matter is that we have been chosen and are responsible to tell people that eternity is coming and they can go into it in relationship either *with* Christ, or *apart* from Him. The responsibility for changing people's minds and/or bringing them to repentance is not in our hands, and for that, we should be eternally thankful to God. However, our compassion for people should *never* wane. It should be the primary reason that drives us onward, knowing that somewhere, in some place, someone will hear the truth and turn to God.

We cannot debate people into a right relationship with God. We cannot argue them into understanding that a certain truth from the Bible is just that. We must always present the truth in gentleness, without all the quarreling (cf. 2 Timothy 2:23-26), that often occurs in the arena of debate.

If we are presenting the truth gently, without quarreling, this precludes debating and arguing. Once a discussion goes beyond instruction, becoming argumentative debate, it ceases to be instruction and becomes counter-productive and senseless.

As human beings, we do not have absolute truth in all things. No one from this life will go to the next to hear Christ say *"Wonderful! You always knew the truth in every area, and expressed it in every nuance!"* That will not happen, which is even more reason to go through this life in humble dependence upon the Holy Spirit, understanding that we will never have perfect knowledge, or will ourselves be perfect in this life.

Chapter 18

Heated Controversies

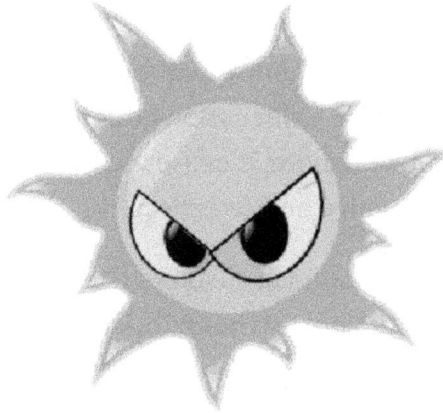

S atan wants us to argue, debate, insult, lord it over others, lie if
necessary, and through innuendo, couch our terms in phrases
that create hurt and tear down, rather than build up. Why?
Because that is what *he* does and he wants us to be like him.

Jesus wants us to go through this life with the humble realization that
without constantly depending upon Him every step of the way, we are in
danger of falling off the humble wagon, thrown to the ground by the
same pride that brought Lucifer to the ground, turning him into the very

tempter of our souls. He wishes nothing but the worst for us and uses every means at his disposal to bring this about. He seeks to destroy and kill.

We are to follow Paul's instructions given to Timothy: *"If someone spreads false teachings and does not agree with sound words (that is, those of our Lord Jesus Christ) and with the teaching that accords with godliness, he is conceited and understands nothing, but has an unhealthy interest in controversies and verbal disputes. This gives rise to envy, dissension, slanders, evil suspicions, and constant bickering by people corrupted in their minds and deprived of the truth, who suppose that godliness is a way of making a profit. Now godliness combined with contentment brings great profit,"* (Timothy 6:3-6, NET).

It is clear that arguments cause division and strife. They are good for nothing, and are generally caused by people who have a very high opinion of themselves. For this reason, they should be avoided.

Paul continues in his second letter to Timothy, saying, *"Remind people of these things and solemnly charge them before the Lord not to wrangle over words. This is of no benefit; it just brings ruin on those who listen. Make every effort to present yourself before God as a proven worker who does not need to be ashamed, teaching the message of truth accurately. But avoid profane chatter, because those occupied with it will stray further and further into ungodliness, and their message will spread its infection like gangrene,"* (2 Timothy 2:14-17, NET). Endlessly arguing or debating about theology is like gangrene. Left unchecked, it will infect the entire local body, passing from one person to the next. It should be avoided. People have a right to disagree. They do not have a right to disagree and disagree and disagree after they have been corrected.

What should our approach be in situations like this? *"And the Lord's slave must not engage in heated disputes but be kind toward all, an apt teacher, patient, correcting opponents with gentleness. Perhaps God will grant them repentance and then knowledge of the truth and they will come to their senses and escape the devil's trap where they are held captive to do his will,"* (2 Timothy 2:24, NET).

Can it be any clearer than what Paul has stated? Here is Paul's list for how the Lord's servant should carry himself in this life:

1. *Do not engage in heated disputes*
2. *Be kind toward all*
3. *Be a good teacher*
4. *Be patient*
5. *Correct opponents with gentleness*
6. *God is the one who grants repentance*
    a. *From repentance comes knowledge of the truth*
    b. *They may come to their senses if they repent*
    c. *They will escape the devil's trap*

We are not Jesus Christ. We do not have His perfection, nor are we able to appropriate His perfection every minute of every day. In eternity, though we will still not be Jesus, the perfection of His human character will be our normal pattern of living, but not in this current reality.

Christ needs to be exalted in everything we do, everything we say, and everything we think. He is not exalted if we are spending our time arguing about this or that. We *must* be able to instruct, using the guidelines set out by the Bible. If, after we have instructed, there is no change in the individual, we must stop arguing with them, while continuing to pray for them, and looking for further opportunities to share the truth with them. God's truth alone causes people to see the need to repent, or it does not, but in either case, we do not bring about repentance. No amount of words – spoken softly or yelled – will cause someone to acknowledge the Truth. It is God's job to do that. Our job is to tell them...*whether they listen or not.*

Resources for Your Library:

BOOKS & DVDs:

- The Antichrist and His Kingdom, by Thomas Ice
- Basis of the Premillennial Faith, The, by Charles C. Ryrie
- Biblical Hermeneutics, by Milton S. Terry
- The Case for Zionism, by Thomas Ice
- Charting the End Times, by LaHaye and Ice
- Christian and Social Responsibility, The, by Charles C. Ryrie
- Church in Prophecy, The by John F. Walvoord
- The Coming Cashless Society, by Thomas Ice and Timothy J Demy
- Dictionary of Premillennial Theology, Mal Couch, Editor
- Dispensationalism Tomorrow & Beyond, by Christopher Cone, Ed
- Exploring the Future, by John Phillips
- Footsteps of the Messiah, by Arnold G. Fruchtenbaum
- Future Israel (Why Christian Anti-Judaism Must Be Challenged), by E. Ray Clendenen, Ed.
- The Great Tribulation, Debate with DeMar and Ice (DVD)
- Interpreting the Bible, by A. Berkeley Mickelsen
- Israelology, by Arnold G. Fruchtenbaum
- Moody Handbook of Theology, The by Paul Enns
- Mountains of Israel, The, by Norma Archbold
- Pre-Wrath Rapture Answered, The, by Lee W. Brainard
- Prolegomena, by Christopher Cone
- Promises of God,The, a Bible Survey, by Christopher Cone
- There Really Is a Difference! by Renald Showers
- Things to Come, by J. Dwight Pentecost
- The Truth Behind Left Behind, by Thomas Ice and Mark Hitchcock
- Truth War, The, by John MacArthur
- What on Earth is God Doing? By Renald Showers

Resources for Your Library (cont'd)

INTERNET:

- Ariel Ministries   www.ariel.org
- Bible Prophecy Today   bible-prophecy-today.blogspot.com/
- Friends of Israel   www.foi.org
- Grace to You   www.gty.org
- Grant Jeffrey Ministries   www.grantjeffrey.com/
- Koinonia House   www.khouse.org/
- PreTrib Rapture Research   www.pre-trib.org/
- Prophecy Central   www.bible-prophecy.com/
- Prophecy in the News   www.prophecyinthenews.com/
- Prophecy Today   www.prophecytoday.com/
- Rapture Ready   www.raptureme.com/
- Rapture Research Website   www.pretribulationrapture.com/
- Rightly Dividing   www.righly-dividing.com
- Study-Grow-Know   www.studygrowknow.com
- Thomas Ice Writings   www.raptureme.com/ttcol.html
- Tyndale Theological Seminary   www.tyndale.edu